THE COLLECTED WRITINGS OF LES RAINEY

VOLUME 1

THE COLLECTED WRITINGS

OF LES RAINEY

VOLUME 1

THE BLESSINGS
OF THE BIBLE

THE BIBLE &
CHRISTIAN DISCIPLINE

THE AMEN GOD

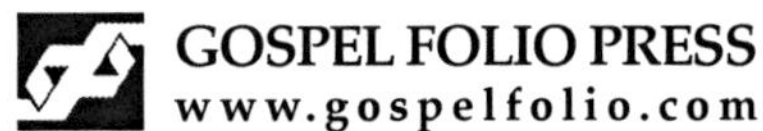

Previously published in three separate volumes:

THE BLESSINGS OF THE BIBLE, first printed by Christian Publications, © February 1988

THE BIBLE AND CHRISTIAN DISCIPLINE

THE AMEN GOD, first printed by M and M Publishers © 1994

THE COLLECTED WRITINGS OF LES RAINEY, VOLUME 1
Les Rainey

Published by
GOSPEL FOLIO PRESS
304 Killaly St. W.
Port Colborne, ON, Canada L3K 6A6
1-800-952-2382
www.gospelfolio.com

Scripture taken from the Authorized King James Version, unless otherwise noted.

ISBN 978-1-897117-29-9

Cover design by Rachel Brooks

Printed in the United States of America.

CONTENTS

THE BLESSINGS OF THE BIBLE

CONTENTS

ONE
THE ORIGIN OF THE WORD "BIBLE"

Why is the Book that has had the greatest moral influence in the world called the "Bible"? It is useful to recall the words from the Coronation Service of Queen Elizabeth II, "The most valuable thing that this world affords … here is wisdom; this is the royal law; these are the lively oracles of God." In the study of the words of the Bible there is none more interesting than that connected with the Book of God. In the museum of Cairo, as well as in the writings of men, we learn that the Bible was written long before printing was invented or paper was discovered. In Southern Asia, and in Egypt, and in the valley of the Jordan, there grew a plant called *papyrus*. The outer covering of this plant was called *biblus*, which was stripped off, put into water, and, after a lengthy process, was formed into parchment. This parchment was tough and flexible and, even with constant use, would last for a hundred years. It was on this parchment that the early prophets wrote the Scriptures.

Then another difficulty arose. As lasting as this parchment was, it would finally wear out. The parchment was glued together in long strips, and then made into a roll. On these rolls the various books of the Bible were written. Being read, studied and handled as they were, these rolls began to wear out. It was then necessary to make copies in order to preserve the written Word. This had to be done by scholars who were experts in language and who understood the message of the prophets who wrote it.

Then a new order of scholars grew up known as the "scribes". Their main duty was to copy the written Books exactly as they had been written and, since they had been educated especially for this service, in the course of time they began to also explain to the people the meaning of the various Books of the Bible. The Books of the Old Testament existed in this parchment form for several hundred years, and new copies were constantly being made to replace the older ones that were wearing out. The scribes were the most learned men of their day.

Let us remember, however, that the scribes did not write the Bible originally. The prophets did that as God revealed Himself and His message to them. But after the prophets were gone, somebody had to look after the parchments, preserve them and re-copy them as needed. And so that class of highly trained men came into existence and were called scribes. These men occupied a high and greatly honoured profession. God's Word was entrusted to their care for many hundreds of years.

Then another thing happened—something quite common in the use of language. The word *biblus*—that is, the name of the parchment on which the words were written—began to be applied to the Sacred Writing itself. Then, since the writings were in rolls of books, the word *biblus* came to mean book.

The Old Testament was written in Hebrew, but the name "Bible" is of Greek origin. This happened in the process of translating the Hebrew into Greek; and through the Latin into English, we have the word Bible, which literally means "book."

If you were to visit a modern bookstore in Jerusalem, Israel, and ask for a Bible, the word used would be "*Tenach*". It is made up of three letters—"T", "N", and "K". These three letters stand for the Torah, the first five books of the Bible; the second letter, N, the prophets; the last letter, K, or our English C—*Coteveem*, meaning "The writings". The Hebrew Bible was arranged in three sections (Luke 24:44).

THE LAW
Genesis, Exodus, Leviticus, Numbers, Deuteronomy.

THE PROPHETS
Joshua, Judges, Samuel, Kings, Isaiah, Jeremiah, Ezekiel and the Twelve Minor Prophets.

THE WRITINGS

Poetical: Psalms, Job, Proverbs.

Rolls (used on special feast days): Song of Solomon, Ruth, Lamentations, Ecclesiastes, Esther.

Non-prophetical: Daniel, Ezra, Nehemiah, Chronicles.

It has always seemed to me that the Old Testament ended on a tragic note of corruption and condemnation, the very opposite of the Book of Revelation. According to the order of the King James Version, this is true, but not according to the Bible of the Jews. The last book of the Hebrew Old Testament is Chronicles, as verified by our Lord in mentioning Abel as the first martyr in Genesis, and Barachias the last in the Book of Chronicles. In Chronicles the nation is visualized going up to Jerusalem and the very words *"let him go up"* (2 Chron. 36:23) are suggestive of worship. Thus, as the New Testament ends on the note of triumph, so the Old Testament concludes with the divine testimony as to the wisdom and knowledge of God and His faithfulness concerning the covenant people known as the Jews.

Though the Bible is composed of many books, it is still one book—"The Book".

The Word of God is unlike all other books; it is a holy Book. It is holy as to its source. *"God hath spoken in His holiness"* (Ps. 60:6). You can search the world and analyze the so-called holy books of religion, but only the Bible can be truthfully called the Holy Bible. It is holy in substance; from cover to cover it is marked by spirituality because of the Holy Spirit of God. Do we not read, *"The Spirit of the Lord spake by me* [David]*"* (2 Sam. 23:2)?

It is holy in speech, because holy men of God spoke as they were moved by the Holy Spirit (2 Pet. 1:21). There is no revelation from God in the works of wicked men. Men such as Shakespeare, Carlisle and Ruskin, have written wise and wonderful words, but none have written about a holy Saviour, a holy calling, a holy name, a holy love and a holy home.

It is holy in sequel, for its ultimate aim is to make holy men and women. God's desire was to make a holy nation, but the nation Israel failed. Now in our generation the purpose of the Holy Spirit is to take out a people for His name, and by His

Spirit make them sanctified vessels useful to Him.

Paul's advice to a young man in 2 Timothy 2:15 defines the high cost of serving God in the sacred Scriptures. Such service will result in a sturdy Christian character, a daily surrendered life, a sanctified course through the world, and a sure and straight presentation of truth in our message. Such a life is influential, invincible and inspirational and has as its incentive that everything in our lives be the exact counterpart of this plan defined in the Scriptures.

If only in our generation, where there is a famine of hearing the Word of God, we might get back to the Book, the basis of all spiritual, national and individual blessing as revealed in the "Oratorio of Scripture" (Ps. 119).

TWO

THE LANGUAGE OF THE BIBLE

The revival of Hebrew, which was no longer in popular use even before the time of Christ, is a remarkable phenomenon. In the early years of the nation of Israel, about one hundred mother tongues were spoken, resulting in linguistic chaos in this miniature united nations state. Now Hebrew is the official language—a living tongue again. The language is logical, pictorial and spiritual.

LOGICAL

Hebrew is one of the most logical languages in the world. Instead of the common perception that it is exceedingly difficult, it is, on the contrary, easy to understand. In English, as well as other languages it is common to use many words, many words are to convey a single idea. In Biblical, as well as in modern, Hebrew such is not the case. Hebrew lends itself to quality rather than quantity, a minimum of words instead of a maximum, reminding one of the amazing brevity and profundity of the greatest of all Hebrew writings, the Scripture of truth. Who else but God could put the message of salvation into a language that would be adaptable to every people under the sun?

PICTORIAL

As you scan the letters that make up the Hebrew alphabet, you quickly discern that they possess names with recognized meanings. A few will suffice as illustrations: an ox, a house, a camel, a hand, an eye, a fish, a serpent; while the last letter of all is Tav—a sacred symbol, or the sign of the Cross. Thus the first and last letters of the Hebrew alphabet are associated with sacrifice. In all the pages of the Bible, by means of these letters, we find portraits of men and women, boys and girls, places and events, of lasting interest. It is like the sun which lightens all lands. Over the centuries, it has spoke to the heart and conscience of every race with crystal clarity and undimmed brilliance.

SPIRITUAL

Perhaps, in the rise of modern Hebrew, there will be research undertaken in relation to the alphabet. To many the origin of the alphabet continues to be a mystery. Yet to the pious Jew, as well as to many scholars in Biblical research, the alphabet is believed to be God-breathed. It is the work of God written in Hebrew, written in Greek, written by the Spirit of God in the language of humanity. The study of such words as God, Jehovah, truth, man, earth, etc., which appear on the threshold of the Bible, are filled with vital, enriching, spiritual depths of knowledge. In approaching the Book, or the fascinating study of its words, there is no wiser counsel than that of the psalmist: *"Open Thou mine eyes, that I may behold wondrous things out of Thy law"* (Ps. 119:18).

THE STUDY OF HEBREW

The Bible is a revelation that yields riches and royalties far beyond our individual capacities. While all cannot be scholars of the Word, we can be among those who meditate upon the Scriptures. I once heard of a simple Christian who had meditated through the Bible three times.

Progress in the knowledge of God does not come through intellectual attainment but, through spiritual adjustment. The Word of God is *"living and powerful"* (Heb. 4:12). Its very words are *"spirit and life"* (John 6:63), and *"light"* (Ps. 119:105), but the prerequisite to revelation is regeneration. C. H. Spurgeon said, "Other books can delight the mind; only this one can quiet the conscience." The wisdom and knowledge of God is not based on innate wisdom but on the indwelling witness of the Holy Spirit of God. Therefore much of the progress in spiritual truth and Christian grace will be dependent on heart searching instead of head studying, communing rather than cramming, humility of spirit rather than highness of soul, and faith rather than facts and figures.

I often used to wonder what words such as Genesis, Exodus, Leviticus, Numbers and Deuteronomy meant, and just where they originated. After spending several years in the land of the Bible and studying the language of the land, I learned that they were words adopted by the translators of the Hebrew Bible into Greek in the days of Alexander the Great. Simply stated, they mean the beginning, the going out, religious exercise, wilderness journeyings and the repeating of the law to the nation Israel.

Going beyond the old Greek version of the Scriptures I learned, the original words of the Hebrew Bible shed new light and beauty on the sacred volume. The very opening word of the Bible is *"in the beginning."* This is the Hebrew word, *beresheet*, and it emphatically states that which is pre-eminent or foremost in time and thought. It contains three words symbolized in the Hebrew letters as "B" meaning son; "R" meaning mind; and "T" meaning cross. Thus the very first word in our Bible contains the revelation of God with every seed or thought of the knowledge and wisdom of the Lord.

The first book of the Bible is not Genesis but *Beresheet*, which, being translated, is *"In the beginning"*. Exodus is rightly rendered, *"These are the names"*, for after the beginning of everything except God, God chooses a people, emancipates and establishes them as sons on the ground of redemption. The third book of the Bible is Leviticus, or *"And He Called"*, immediately taking us into the sanctuary, where we learn something of the holiness of God and our relationship in worship. Numbers simply means *"in the wilderness"*, and so vividly points out the problems, perils and privileges of all who walk through the desert sands and howling waste wilderness. The fifth book of the Pentateuch, Deuteronomy, like all other books of the Bible, has the key right inside the door—*"These be the words"* (Deut. 1:1). This book emphasizes the truth of God's Word to a new and rising generation. How fitting this title in view of the fact that our Lord quotes three times from it in His temptation in the wilderness. What is seen in relation to the opening books of the Bible is systematically followed all the way through from Genesis to Revelation. For all and any who are diligent, and will take time, God is faithful in the communicating of His mind and will.

THREE
WHAT THE BIBLE IS CALLED

ITS SOURCE—TO BE RECEIVED
1. "The words of God" (Ps. 107:11; 1 Thess. 2:13)
   "The book" (Luke 4:20)
   "The book of the Law" (Gal. 3:10)
   From Psalm 19:7-9 note:
   "The law of the Lord"
   "The testimony of the Lord"
   "The statutes of the Lord"
   "The commandment of the Lord"
   "The fear of the Lord"
   "The judgments of the Lord"

ITS AUTHORITY—TO BE UPHELD
2. *"The word of a King"* (Eccl. 8:4)

ITS CHARACTER—TO BE REVEALED
3. *"The words of the Holy One"* (Job 6:10)

ITS INSPIRATION—TO BE REVERED
4. *"words of His mouth"* (Job 23:12; Isa. 55:11)

ITS FINALITY—TO BE STUDIED
5. *"The word of truth"* (Jas. 1:18)

ITS RELIABILITY—TO BE HELD

    6.   *"The faithful word"* (Titus 1:9)

ITS MESSAGE—TO BE DECLARED

    7.   *"The word of Thy righteousness"* (Ps. 119:123)
        "The word of promise" (Rom. 9:9)
        "The word of His grace" (Acts 14:3; 20:32)
        "The word of reconciliation" (2 Cor. 5:19)
        "The word of life" (Phil. 2:16)
        "The word of My patience" (Rev. 3:10)
        "The sword of the Spirit" (Eph. 6:17)
        "The faith once for all delivered to the saints" (Jude 3)
        "The oracles of God" (Rom. 3:2; Heb. 5:12)
        "The lively (living) oracles" (Acts 7:38)
        "The holy scriptures" (Rom. 1:2)
        "The scriptures of the prophets" (Rom. 16:26)
        "The scriptures of truth" (Dan. 10:21)
        "The word of God" (Heb. 4:12)
        "The word of the Lord" (1 Pet. 1:25)
        "The word of Christ" (Col. 3:16)
        "The word of the gospel" (Acts 15:7)
        "The word of this salvation" (Acts 13:26)
        "The word of the cross" (1 Cor. 1:18, RV)

PSALM 119

The author of the Holy Scriptures, like the Creator in nature, reveals His perfection in the use of certain words and phrases in the one hundred and nineteenth Psalm. In this chapter there are 176 verses divided into twenty-two sections. Each group has eight verses. The number eight conveys the thought of more than enough. Since there are twenty-two letters in the Hebrew alphabet we are reminded of the 22 skull bones, and surely this is not mere chance but design, skill, order, and perfection. God's desire is that we might know His mind and heart. It is for this purpose that ten synonyms for the Word of God are employed by the Holy Spirit in the alphabet of divine love: 1. Law; 2. Testimonies; 3. Ways; 4. Precepts; 5. Statutes; 6. Commandments; 7.

Judgment; 8. Word; 9. Sayings; 10. Righteousness.

1. Law (*torah*) is a word greatly revered by the Jew and always used in the singular. The root is most suggestive, meaning to propel or project as an arrow from a bow. An arrow warped in the making is never true in its flight. This was in the mind of the writer in Psalm 19, where we are told the law of the Lord is perfect, converting the soul. It signifies direction, destiny and God's decalogue as the rule of life.

2. Testimonies (*eduth*) suggests reiteration, or testimony and reminds us of the witness of the altar in Joshua 22:34. The motive of the two and a half tribes in establishing the altar "Ed" was not disloyalty, but an external proof of the theocracy of the nation. The outcome of the meeting with the other tribes was the prevention of civil war, the perpetuity of mutual relationships as tribes, and a practical lesson for Christians of all generations concerning misunderstandings. What a testimony to the truth of Psalm 133!

3. Ways (*derek*) signifies a footpath, a common path pointing to a given destination, and implies a mode of life, a fixed course for the journey of life along which we are to walk in obedience to God's Word.

4. Precepts (*piqqudim*) is derived from a root meaning to visit, to inspect or oversee, to charge, and since it is always used in the plural, denotes intensity, purpose of heart, moral earnestness relative to the mandates of the Book of God.

5. Statutes (*chuqqim*) comes from a root meaning "graven" or to hew, to cut-in, inscribe, engrave and usually rendered statute or decree. Thus what God has ordained, decreed, prescribed, should be permanently engraved on our hearts and brains in order that the Word of God might become flesh (John 1:14), and His people translated as enduring epistles (2 Cor. 3:1-3).

6. Commandments (*mitsvah*) is an interesting word meaning to set up, to constitute, and often used as a definite charge backed by authority. To refuse to obey is an act of rebellion. God's commands are never given without the power to carry them out, therefore all His commandments are His enablings and for our enjoyment.

7. Judgments (*mishpatim*) takes us into the law court and means to give a finding which is just, upright and true, coming from a root meaning to set up right. Judgment, therefore, denotes the verdict of God. God's findings are final. How often in the Prophets He speaks by means of a vision, then a voice resulting in a verdict (see Joel chapters 1-3, Vision, Voice and Verdict). His wise and just decisions are not to be questioned, denied or distorted, but to be accepted, loved and followed.

8.   **Word (*dabar*)**, meaning to set forth in speech. It is the articulation of the will of God in the language of holy love. To follow His word, His promise, His message, is the pathway to purity within (v. 9) and power without (v. 11).

9.   **Sayings (*imrah*)** means an utterance and is different in meaning from the word found in verses 11, 38, 41, 50, 58, 67, 76, 82, 103, 116, 123, 133, 140, 148, 154, 158, 162, 170, 172. It signifies revelation and illumination as an utterance which conveys the thought of the speaker. How significant this word in view of the title applied to Christ! "The Logos" or the "Word of God". How much we should value the sayings of the Saviour, the very breath of God.

10. **Righteousness (*tzaddi*)** is derived from a root meaning "justice" or "right". The inherent meaning is right, true, just, and is used for "just balances" in Leviticus 19:36. God's Word is the standard of measurement by which all our actions are weighed or lined.

Thus these ten words taken together by a nation, community or a child of God will result in lasting blessing to the individual and the benediction of heaven to all—regardless of class, colour or country.

FOUR

IS THE BIBLE TRUSTWORTHY FOR TODAY?

Seldom a week passes but what I am in conversation with someone who flatly asserts that the Bible is nothing more than a human book, subject to earthly limitations, and revered only by the minority. There are others who tell us that the Bible is the book of God, but they go on to state that we cannot trust all of its statements. When it speaks of spiritual matters, they assure us, we may trust it, but when it comes to the things of science or space, history or geography, it cannot be considered inerrant or infallible.

As a Christian, how blessed it is to place one's confidence in the words of the Holy Scriptures, which are able *"to make one wise unto salvation through faith which is in Jesus Christ."* As long as life shall last and time moves on towards the fulfilment of all God's purposes, the God-breathed Book and those who believe will be subject to more and more animosity and attacks. Yet in the midst of all it can be, as it was to the champion of the Reformation: "The Holy Scriptures are to believing souls what the meadow is to the ox, what the home is to the man, what the nest is to the bird, the stream to the fish, and the cleft of the rock to the seafowl."

If it is only the work of men, we can never lean on it for spiritual support. If it is no more than a product of a human brain, it must be a compilation of human ideas about morality and ethics, with a smattering of Jewish background as history. But it is more than this—it is inspired by God.

There are two words to note in the gift of the Bible. The first is "revelation" and the second is "inspiration". Both are basically Latin words. The first simply means to uncover, to unveil, to reveal from *"revelo"*, from which we get our word revelation. The Latin word meaning to breathe into is *"inspiro"*, from which we get our word inspiration. In writing to Timothy, Paul makes two assertions about the Scripture (2 Tim. 3:16). He speaks of all Scriptures as being inspired and as being profitable. Paul's language was Greek and he combines God and breath to give us *"theoneustos"*. The Greek word *theos*, God, is found in theology, theophany, atheist, Dorothy, Theodore; the word *pneuma*, breath, is found in pneumatic (for tires with air or a drill run by compressed air), and pneumonia (a disease of the lungs). These two words put together give us *"theopneustos"* which is found only here in the Bible. The God-breathed word *"theopneustos"* is exactly that—God-breathed. It suggests a flutist playing his instrument by breathing into it. Just as God created man by breathing into him the breath of life so that he became *"a living soul"*, so God breathed into the writers of the Bible so that each could write the Holy Scriptures. How foolish it is to think the men who wrote the Bible were inspired men. It is what they wrote or their writings which were inspired. Even though Moses lost his temper and killed a man, that does not militate against the fact that he wrote the Pentateuch, which is the inspired five books of Moses. God spoke through men, and these writings have been preserved by God down through the centuries until this day.

It was rather a spiritual shake-up to me when I was asked, "Do you believe every word in the Bible is true?" "Of course," I answered. Some men have actually taught this, but the Bible does not so teach. The Bible is a record of facts and revelation of God. If someone in the Bible tells a lie, it is recorded as a lie; the truth is that the lie was told. The Bible contains many stories of faithless human beings whose deeds were likewise faithless. The Bible assures us of the accuracy of the Bible accounts. It does not mean that God approves the utterances or deeds of the characters in a particular story.

For example, in the Book of Job we read, *"Skin for skin, all that a man has he will give in exchange for his life"* (Job 2:4). That sentence is serpent-like. It is simply not true. If we read the context carefully, we discover that that lie was spoken by the devil himself, for he is the father of lies. What is true and inspired is that the devil told that lie while reporting to God about his dealings with Job.

So inspiration carries absolute accuracy as to the historicity of the narratives, but lends no authority to the speech and behaviour of the sinful beings who walk through its pages. On the other hand, where God speaks directly in Scripture, there is not only complete accuracy, but also absolute authority. Again and again, whether in the first chapter of Genesis or the last chapter of Malachi, the expression *"And God said"* is found, or its equivalent, over 3,000 times, confirming that the message is not human opinion but divine revelation.

In my study of the Bible I have never felt it adequate enough to tell my friends I believe its message because I was brought up in a Christian home and was taught the words of God as a child. Such is not very convincing to the sceptics, the scorners, the open-minded or the liberal-minded. Many want to know if the Bible is fact or fiction, true or false, or relevant for the world of today.

For years, whether at home or on the road with the message of life, there is one book that has always been an encouragement to my soul—it is the Book of the Psalms. When it comes to the absolute assurance and authority of the Scriptures there are three psalms devoted to extolling God's Word. Psalm 1 shows the prosperity of its devout, devoted reader (vv. 1-3), his fruitfulness and blessedness of life being contrasted with the worthlessness and perishing life of the ungodly (vv. 4-6). In each case the similes are drawn from nature. Psalm 19 also divides into three parts and bids us look to the skies, the Scriptures and the soul. The whole psalm is a revelation of religion in three aspects: Natural Theology (1-6), Revealed Theology (7-11) and Practical Theology (12-14). God has not left Himself without witness, and in the skies we have revealed His works; in the Scriptures His words, and in the soul His witnesses. In the central section there are six titles of His Book all linked to the "Lord", their source and center. The six qualities are summed up in the first—"perfect"—for the Bible is pre-eminent over all other books. The results are not only relative to the present but into the future, for if these words are graven on the heart, and their message received, it means blessing now and everlasting benediction for the hereafter.

The final psalm to which we call attention is 119, the longest chapter in the Bible. It follows an exact structural scheme—the alphabet. Does God press His message into such a seemingly artificial mould? Yes, as much as to say, "My Word is the universal language to the human heart; beyond it there is nothing of truth for speech to utter." There is one phrase which expresses the unity of the Bible, and that expression occurs thirty-five times in Psalm 119; namely, "Thy Word". This is in the singular number, and accords with a common usage in the book. Think of it, there are three times thirteen books in the Old Testament, and three times nine books in the New Testament—sixty-six books in all, or three times twenty-two books. Surely it is not without divine purpose that man is so constituted as to have 22 skull bones. God's design is that we might know Him and our desire should be, "Give me the Bible, the whole Bible, and nothing but the Bible, as authority and chart on life's voyage from time to eternity."

In this alphabet of divine love and learning we have the inexhaustible fullness of the Word of God and all that it can be to man the creature of the day. There are three references to the eternal character of the Word of God (Ps. 119:89, 152 and 160).

1. THE WORD IS FOREVER SETTLED

What does it mean that the Word of God is forever settled? Surely it has reference to now, today, the present. The Bible is relevant for the world in which we live and labour, plant and build, woo and warn, sow and serve until He come. The Hebrew root signifies that it has been set up, it stands upright, like a pillar that cannot be moved. There in heaven God's Word has been established forever. It is unchangeable, unshaken, eternal as the throne of God. Dictators and earthly rulers make decrees and, as long as they are in power, they stand. Yet they change and are often revoked; they do not prevail, and finally perish, but the Word of the Lord endures forever. The word of God links us with eternity past and on into the eternity of tomorrow, and here in the present our confidence is, "What saith the Scriptures?" What security for the believer in an age of superficiality and false claims of men whose breath is in their nostrils! It's no wonder we sing:

> The B-I-B-L-E,
> Yes, that's the Book for me;
> I stand alone on the Word of God:
> The B-I-B-L-E.

2. THE WORD FOUNDED FOREVER

Again we are linked with the past. The Hebrew word means to lay a foundation. It is used of the founding of the earth, *"The Lord by wisdom hath founded the earth"* (Prov. 3:19); *"The earth is the Lord's ... for He hath founded it"* (Ps. 24:1-2). Our age is one in which the foundations of morality are being shaken. As never before restraint is being cast off, and when the Bible is discredited, denied and defied as God's standard, what can be done? Rest secure on the inspired, immutable and inerrant Word of God. We are no more left without a foundation of moral and spiritual principles from God than we are left without changeless natural laws.

3. THE WORD WILL ENDURE FOREVER

Not only the psalmist but the great evangelical prophet as well as the apostle of hope rise up to tell us the Word of God shall stand forever (Isa. 40:8; 1 Pet. 1:23). Not only did our Lord quote from at least 24 books of the Old Testament, but He affirmed, *"Verily I say unto you, till heaven and earth pass, one jot or one tittle shall in no wise pass from the law, till all be fulfilled"* (Matt. 5:18). He quoted or referred to Daniel 22 times, Isaiah 40 times, the Pentateuch 60 times, with never a hint that He did not regard the persons mentioned as real, historic persons. In Luke 24:27, 44 Jesus claimed Himself to be a subject of prophecy and all through the Old Testament. Was He deceived in this claim? Impossible, if He was the sinless Son of God. Was He deceiving Himself, knowing better but pretending this to be true? Impossible, for the same reason. Listen to His claim: *"Heaven and earth shall pass away: but My words shall not pass away"* (Mark 13:31). When the world is burned up in that future day there in heaven will stand the eternal living Word, a pillar to the faithfulness of God, forever settled, forever founded, forever enduring. Another wonderful feature of this psalm, often overlooked by the casual reader of Scripture, is the fact that the 176 verses are divided into twenty-two sections which, of course, correspond to the Hebrew alphabet. Each group has eight verses. There are twenty-two letters, and each section commences with one of the letters of the alphabet, so there is one letter for each group. This may be seen in an ordinary Bible, as the letter is spelled out over each section. "Aleph" is over the first, "Beth" is over the second section. Over the section of verse 89 is the letter "L", which signifies an "ox-goad"; over the section containing verse 152 is the letter "Q", symbolising the back of a man's head; verse 160 comes under a section which is very clear, the letter "R", which represents the mind. Thus it is the design of God the Spirit that the truth of these words—forever settled; forever founded, and will endure forever—be as a goad or prick that we might never forget the mind and will of God.

> The earth shall pass away, some day,
> But My Word shall not pass away.
> The sun may fade, the moon decay,
> But God's Word lives forever.
>
> The flags of nations may be furled,
> The mountains to the seas be hurled,
> One thing will still outlast the world,
> God's Word shall live forever!

FIVE

THE SUFFICIENCY OF THE SCRIPTURES
JAMES 1:18-25

The book of James certainly reveals the value and virtue of the Word of God. As a writer he was saturated with the Scriptures, and not only does he make mention of vivacious personalities, and various passages of the Old Testament, but also periodicals of his times, such as the Apocrypha. Reading it through one does not need to be a scholar to see how readily it reflects the Sermon on the Mount. It is no wonder it is given the Canadian title "Faith in Overalls", and the Southern U.S.A. title, "A Belief that Behaves". There are four titles in these verses revealing the systematic and experimental fullness of the Bible.

FINALITY

The first title is most suggestive in bringing before us two words—"Logos" and "Truth". It is not the regular word used for articulation, but a divine title of revelation concerning the Lord Jesus Christ. How blessed to note here that Christ is the alphabet of God, the spokesman from heaven, the transmitter of the truth of God. The original language (Hebrews) reveals that the word "Logos" is made up of three letters—"D", "B" and "R". The first means door, and Christ was the Door to the living and true God, opening up the way to the understanding of the Father's heart. He was the One who came from heaven as told out in the second letter, meaning "home". Finally, the letter "R" is the symbol of the head and suggests the mind and will of God. So Christ came to tell out finally and fully the mind and heart of God. The word truth is also most suggestive in the

Hebrew tongue. It contains the first, the last and middlemost letters of the Hebrew alphabet. The truth is first and will be last, and combines all extremes and unites all ends. It is easier for the heavens and the earth to pass away than for one tittle of truth to fail. Christ came into the world and announced He was the Truth and apart from Him there is no going, knowing or growing in the fullness and finality of truth.

VITALITY

The second title used by James is the word "engrafted", which is rendered "implanted". The Word of God is likened to a "seed" with its life-giving power to produce. The context reveals that there must be suitable soil for the seed. We must lay aside *"all filthiness and abounding of wickedness"* (DARBY) and this can only be done by the infusion of a new power, a new life. The stem of our old natural Adamic life is not suitable to God. He must engraft His Word and thereby infuse His divine life. The word "implanted" teaches us the inwardness of the operation of the Word and work of God. His Word is life-giving in power. Not only is it living, but powerful or able to save the soul. The Word of God effectually operates in the soul of the one who believes, reproducing the very life of God. The Word of God becomes flesh and expresses itself in word and deed in a world of dead sinners. Oh to be like the early Christians and to receive it with meekness, to follow on to practice it in doctrine, fellowship, breaking of bread and prayers (Acts 2:41-42).

REALITY

1.   The story is told of a missionary who dropped a small mirror in the African jungle. A member of a primitive tribe picked it up and eagerly took it home, gazing into it all the way. "Why," he exclaimed to his wife, "I've found a picture of my father just as he used to be years ago." His wife took it and looked into it. "This isn't your father, it's a very ugly woman." In the Bible we see ourselves as we really are.

2.   "It is not enough to remember what we hear, and to be able to repeat it, and to give testimony to it, and commend it and write it, and preserve what we have written; but that which

is required of us, and which crowns the rest, is that we be doers of the Word" (Matthew Henry).

3. The next reference to the Bible is, the hearing and doing of the Word of God. It is not enough to hear only. We must practice the truth of God. The Bible is to become our measure and model of character and conduct. Many in James' day were accustomed to listen to lectures in the public squares or in the Greek schools of learning. Various topics of the day were discussed but they were quickly forgotten. However, one may easily lose the fleeting impressions and words of a speaker, yet to forget the words of God is to be in jeopardy of losing life. Man is so constituted that he cannot possibly live by physical bread only. He needs the Bread of God, which alone can originate, sustain and satisfy eternal life. James warns that we are not to be deceived by failing to apply the truth of God to our own personal lives. It has been said: "Some books inform, others reform, but only the Bible transforms." When a man refuses to put into practice what he has been taught, he is like a man seeing his face in a mirror but immediately forgetting what he saw. The mirror shows what is wrong and something must be done. We are not to come carelessly or casually to the Bible, but with concentrated gaze to prove what Paul taught. *"But we all, with open face beholding as in a glass the glory of the Lord, are changed into the same image from glory to glory, even as by the Spirit of the Lord"* (2 Cor. 3:18).

AUTHORITY

The last picture of the Bible in this illuminating passage is the *"perfect law of liberty"* (James 1:25). The Word of God is likened to a mirror. The Old Testament was God's voice to the nation, but it was weak through the flesh (Rom. 8:3). In the New Testament age of grace we have the Holy Spirit who has come to convict and comfort. The Word of God is given also to convict, convert, cleanse, consecrate and comfort. What was impossible under the law is now able to be performed according to the Spirit. What a paradox we have here! Law imposes restraint. Yet here we find the phrase, *"law of liberty"*. While the Spirit of God constrains, He also restrains. Not only does He direct, but He deters and drives as we see in the life of our Lord (Luke 4 and Acts 16). Not only do we have the motivating, restraining influence of the Word of God, but we also note its perfection and authority in the words of this title.

> Behold the book whose leaves display
> Jesus the Life, the Truth, the Way,
> Read it with diligence and prayer,
> Search it and thou shalt find Him there.

In summing up, how blessed to see we have the legacy of life, light and liberty in Christ through the Scriptures. The Bible is a revealer of God, self and stewardship. It is to be our molder and model in Christian character and conduct. For time and for eternity our attitude should be receptive, reflective, retentive, that heavenly precepts may be turned into daily practice as long as life shall last.

SIX

THE SYMBOLS OF THE BIBLE

ITS INDIVIDUALITY

The Bible is unique for its universality as well as its individuality. It is one of the wonders of time in the marvellous way in which it was formulated, compiled and completed. Reaching over a period of 1,600 years, written by various people and in a variety of places, it comprises 66 books, yet one Book.

> Whence but from heaven could men unskilled in arts,
> In several ages born, in several parts,
> Weave such agreeing truths? Or how, or why,
> Should all conspire to cheat us with a lie?

There is no book so personal, for it is the message of God's heart to the heart of man.

ITS INDESTRUCTIBILITY

For years it has been the anvil on which the hammers of the enemy have been worn out. Though the object of satanic hatred in all ages, it still stands in solitary majesty, "The Everlasting Word". Eighteen centuries have passed since the Word of God was completed. During these years change after change has taken place but the Bible is still the same, yesterday, today and forever, *settled in heaven* (Ps. 119:89). Even today, after copyings almost innumerable and after being tossed about through ages of ignorance and tumult, the text of Holy Writ is found to be unaltered as to every important doctrine. Well can we respond to the language of Isaiah, *The grass withereth, the flower fadeth; but the word of our God shall stand forever* (40:8).

ITS INCOMPARABILITY

The Bible is not to be placed on the same plane as the great works of literature. The God-breathed Book is alone and aloof in the dignity of inspiration.

(A) Its scope. It reaches the frontiers of civilization and its voice is heard throughout the ends of the earth. It is read by the poet and the philosopher, the statesman and the servant, the rich and the poor, the learned and the ignorant, and is accessible to the hand and heart of man the world over.

(B) Its sale. It is the most popular book on the shelf, counter or library—the greatest seller of all, and will be as long as time shall continue.

ITS SYMBOLS

From Genesis to Revelation the Bible speaks for itself and does not require the seal of man. There are many figures of the Word of God and below are listed a number for our profit and study:

1. The Bible is an Adjuster (2 Tim. 3:16)
2. The Bible is a Builder (Acts 20:32; Jude 20)
3. The Bible is a Comforter (Rom. 15:4)
4. The Bible is a Fire (Jer. 23:29, cf Jer. 20:9)
5. The Bible is a Hammer (Jer. 23:9 cf John 16:7-11)
6. The Bible is a Lamp (Ps. 119:105; 2 Pet. 1:19)
7. The Bible is a Light (Ps. 119:105)
8. The Bible is the Word of Life (Phil. 2:16; Heb. 4:12; 1 Pet. 1:23-25)
9. The Bible is Milk (Heb. 5:12; 1 Pet. 2:2)
10. The Bible is Meat (Heb. 5:12)
11. The Bible is a Mirror (Jas. 1:25; 2 Cor. 3:18)
12. The Bible is Seed (Luke 8:11; 1 Pet. 1:23)
13. The Bible is a Sword (Eph. 6:17; Heb. 4:12)
14. The Bible is Water (Eph. 5:26; John 15:3; John 17:17)

These various symbols demonstrate the fullness we have to meet our every need from guilt to glory, from the city of destruction to the city of God.

For:

(1) The Word of God as an **Adjuster** equips us for salvation, sanctification and service. "It is different from any other book in that it suits all times and circumstances, adapting itself to youth, to maturity and to old age, being the comfort in affliction, the guide in darkness, the joy in adversity and the companion in prosperity."

(2) The Word of God as a **Lamp** for our feet and light for our path reveals to us where to go and where not to go. Many commentators have pointed out that the feeble lanterns which men carry throw a circle around their feet and illumine the distance of a single step; nevertheless that is all that is needed for walking in darkness. A man who is walking on a mountain path need not see the bottom of every canyon or the summit of every peak. If he can see where he is to take his next step, he will find the way home. This is what the Bible does for God's people.

(3) The Word of God as a **Fire** consumes, comforts and confirms. This fire keeps us warm in a cold and complex world and at the same time burns out the dross so easily absorbed by the Lord's own people.

(4) The Word of God is like a **Hammer** that breaks and builds. In Jeremiah, God is speaking to false prophets who prophesy in the name of the Lord but do not prophesy what the Lord wants His people to know. God says that He hates false preaching, and tells His people that His Word, like a fire and hammer, will burn and break all who speak contrary to Him. His Word will be the standard of judgment. The Word of God first convicts us, then breaks us up, and finally builds us up in our most holy faith.

(5) The Word of God as a **Sword** is to be used by us to defend ourselves against the triple foe of the believer. It pierces, protects, and is powerful in the conflict of the Christian. The Lord met the attack of the enemy with the flashing sword: *"It is written …"* The same weapon is ours to wield, and enables us to carry the battle into the camp of the evil one (Eph. 6:17).

(6) The Word of God describes itself as a **Diet** for digestion, development and discretion. As honey it speaks of sweetness and satisfaction. As water it cleanses and consecrates from

all defilement. As milk and meat it develops and determines growth and godliness. When we come to Christ we need simple teaching—the milk. But after we acquire assurance we must study the great truths of the Scriptures in order to attain to the stature of the fullness of Christ (Eph. 4:13). As new-born babes we long for the pure, personal milk of the Word (1 Pet. 2:2), but we must grow up to the solid food in order to be spiritually strong (Heb. 5:12).

(7) The Word of God as a **Mirror** shows us what we are and what we ought to be like. No doubt this is why the Bible is the most hated book in the world as well as the most loved. This reminds me of a cartoon of an over-weight woman carrying the bathroom scales to the attic, where they could be out of sight, as well as an African who, viewing himself for the first time in a mirror, promptly smashed it into a hundred pieces. Removing the scales or breaking the mirror does not remove a single wrinkle or improve the countenance. The mirror of the Word of God shows every man his inner being. Happy is the man who can say, "I have seen myself in the mirror of the Word of God. I recognize that the horrid image is myself as God sees me. I have accepted God's invitation to turn from the mirror to the fountain of Calvary, where Christ has provided full and free cleansing for me." The wonderful thing about the mirror is that if we turn to Christ, when we turn back to the mirror we discover that we have been made like Christ and that one day we shall awake in His likeness forever.

Adjuster, light, lamp, fire, hammer, sword, diet, milk, meat, scalpel, seed, fine gold, critic! What an amazing book! It is the wonderful Word of the living God ! How clearly it reveals in every part that it has been written by God! *"It is written..."* This is our life and authority. Years ago William Kelly wrote, "As the end draws near we do greatly need simplicity to rest upon God's Word. It is only in the Bible that we have the divine revelation of the heart and mind of God to a rebel race."

AN APPRECIATION OF THE BIBLE BY S. CHADWICK

I have worked at the Bible, prayed over the Bible, lived by the Bible for more than sixty years, and I tell you there is no book like the Bible. It is a miracle of literature, a perennial spring of wisdom, a wonder book of surprises, a revelation of mystery, an infallible guide of conduct, and an unspeakable source of comfort. Give no heed to people that discredit it, for they speak without knowledge. It is the Word of God in the inspired speech of humanity. Read it for yourself. Read it through. Study it according to its own directions. Live by its principles. Believe its message. Follow its precepts.

No man is uneducated who knows the Bible, and no man is wise who is ignorant of its teaching. Every day is begun at its open pages. It lies close at hand in all my work. I never go anywhere without it and it is my chief joy.

I am pleading, therefore, for a return to a painstaking study of the Bible; that is, to put into the study of the Bible the same concentration and work as we must put into our science textbook or our language primer. It means hard work. Bible study is study, as Archbishop Trench wrote: 'Holy Scripture is not a book for the slothful. It is a field, rather, upon the surface of which sometimes we gather manna easily and without labour, giving, as it were, freely to our hands; yet of which many portions are to be cultivated with pains and toil ere they yield food for the service of man.'

In the words of Canon Hague: "Therefore, think not of it as a good book, or even as a better book, but lift it in heart and mind and love far, far above all, and ever regard it, not as the word of man, but as it is in truth, the Word of God; nay, more, as the living Word of the Living God; supernatural in origin; eternal in duration; inexpressible in value; infinite in scope; divine in authorship; human in penmanship; regenerative in power; infallible in authority; universal in interest; personal in application and, as St. Paul declares, inspired in totality."

SEVEN

HOW TO READ THE BIBLE
NEHEMIAH 8:1-18

The chapter before us tells the happenings of a week (v. 18), and what a week it was! The people asked for the Word of God and, under the ministry of His servant, they got it. To Nehemiah and the people of his day it was a living Book and contained the power to give life. It is profitable for teaching, for conviction, for restoration and for education in righteousness. It is God's revelation of the fullness of His love through Christ. It strengthens. It encourages. It comforts. It challenges. It discerns the thoughts and intents of the heart. It is God's Book, the Bible. Our motto should be *homo unius libri*—a man of one Book.

1. THE REQUEST FOR THE BOOK (8:1-7)

The people asked for the book and they were given it. Note the Place, the Pulpit, the People. It was in a public place and by the Water Gate. Ezra, taught and trained of God in the Scriptures, stood on a pulpit. Then he led in worship and in fellowship with others, and brought before them the words of God. The people were attentive to hear the Word, and showed reverence in standing up.

2. HOW TO READ THE BIBLE (8:8, 18)

In the study of this chapter we have already seen that there was a definite time of preparation. In any genuine work of God there must be the searching of the Scriptures. At times I have almost imagined I could hear Ezra and his colleague Nehemiah. They read the Word of God, not as some do when they gabble it, drone it or half swallow their words, but **(a) distinctly, (b)**

discerningly; that is, in plain terms, what it really says. It was the exposition of the Word for the heart, and not merely the head. **(c) Daily,** if not in public, certainly in private.

One of the most illuminating experiences in my attendance in the synagogues of Jerusalem was the public reading of the Scriptures. There were laws laid down for the habitual reading of the Word of God and the language was considered by far the best and purest Hebrew. While preaching or teaching was entirely optional, the reading of the Scriptures was obligatory. How often in various places of worship, when sheep come together to be fed, the Bible is not even opened and read, let alone expounded.

Some time ago I read seven good reasons why the Bible should be read in public. One is that the Scriptures are holy, in and by themselves separate from surroundings. Second, they are perfectly profitable in themselves. Third, they have perfect concord and harmony with themselves. Fourth, they convey an admirable force in the proper reading. Fifth, there is great plainness and easiness of style in the Word of God. Sixth, there is a gracious simplicity and impartiality in the Scripture presentations of truth. And last of all, God's own Spirit works in and through the Scriptures.

Perhaps one of the failures in the daily systematic reading of the Sacred Oracles is that we put too much emphasis on our interpretation rather than dependence on the Spirit of God. If the Holy Spirit is a living, pulsating force in our lives then the Bible will be a living revelation rather than a record of historical events. Dwelling in the land and the study of the Hebrew tongue has forever implanted in my heart the reality and freshness of the Bible for today's world.

Familiarize yourself with the history; get into the scene yourself; get all the sidelights you can from topography, and geography, and botany, and chemistry, and geology, and everything else that will throw light upon the exact condition of things. When, for instance, you read of the lilies of the field, and the sparrows, you should know how these appear to an Eastern mind. You need to understand the outward appearance of the lily, which is not white but scarlet, with a hood like a canopy over a throne, and therefore it presented a striking illustration of Solomon in his scarlet robes, with a canopy over his head. Such research will help you wonderfully to a true exposition of the Scripture.

HOW TO READ THE BIBLE

> Read the Bible, not as a newspaper, but as a home letter. If a cluster of heavenly fruit hangs within reach, gather it. If a promise lies upon a page as a blank cheque, cash it. If a prayer is recorded, appropriate it and launch it as a feathered arrow from the bow of your desire.
>
> If an example of holiness gleams before you, ask God to do as much for you.
>
> If the truth is revealed in all its intrinsic splendour, entreat that its brilliance may ever irradiate the hemisphere of your life.
>
> —F. B. Meyer

The Bishop of Durham wrote many years ago: "I place, of course, the secret study of the holy written Word of God supreme among the helps to secret prayer. Read the Bible on your knees, at least on the knees of your spirit. Read it to reassure, to regulate, to feed, to kindle, to give your secret prayer body and soul. Read it that you may hold fast your certainty of being heard. Read it that you may know with blessed definiteness whom you have believed, and what you have in Him, and how He is able to keep your deposit safe. Read it in the attitude of mind which the Apostles read it, in which the Lord read it."

In response to the questioning of a young Christian who earnestly confided to G. R. Harding Wood, of Great Britain, that he found the Bible dull, Mr. Wood came forth with a splendid yet simple answer centering around four of the many relationships the believer entered into with the Lord Jesus Christ at the moment of salvation. To all, whether or not this young person's problem has been yours as well, he has suggested that we should read the Bible:

1. **Completely,** as part of the bride of Jesus (just as a bride reads a love letter).

2. **Constantly,** as a traveller to the home of Jesus.
3. **Carefully,** as a scholar in the school of Jesus.
4. **Conscientiously,** as a soldier in the army of Jesus.

Reading the Bible slowly, reverently and prayerfully, it can be covered in a year by doing two chapters in the Old Testament and one in the New Testament every week day, and two of the New Testament on Sundays. Here is a schedule that has helped me over the years.

Month	Morning	Noon	Night
Jan.	Genesis	Psalm 1 to 41	Matthew
Feb.	Exodus	Psalm 42 to 72	Mark
March	Leviticus	Psalm 73 to 106	Luke
April	Numbers	Psalm 107 to 150	John
May	Deuteronomy	Proverbs	Acts
June	Joshua to Ruth	Ecclesiastes and Song of Solomon	Romans
July	1 Samuel	Isaiah	1 Corinthians
August	2 Samuel	Jeremiah and Lamentations	2 Corinthians
Sept.	1 and 2 Kings	Ezekiel	Galatians and Ephesians
Oct.	1 Chronicles	Daniel to Amos	Philippians to Philemon
Nov.	2 Chronicles	Obadiah to Malachi	Hebrews to 2 Peter
Dec.	Ezra to Esther	Job	1 John to Revelation

The great secret of good public reading of the Scriptures is naturalness, as opposed to artificiality. How difficult this is when facing a large audience, sympathetic or otherwise! To speak in the language of the people with ease and simplicity one must be among the people and at home with them. Wherever the Lord went and spoke the words of truth, it was with the breath of God, and all His words are marked with brevity and beauty. All the recorded words of Christ could be printed in a 16-page pamphlet. His longest speech takes but fifteen minutes to read aloud. You could never imagine the Lord hurrying and lifting up His voice to shout or scream. Isaiah tells us of His dignity and quietness of speech (Isa. 42:2). How important to observe the pause in reading, so common in the Hebrew Bible. This is seen in the very opening words of the Bible. In the account of creation in Genesis 1, any possible length of time may have intervened between the events referred to in the first verse and those in the second. *"In the beginning God created the heavens and the earth."* Here a pause may follow, to intimate a break in the continuity of events, and after a short interval the reader may resume. To have the proper rate of speaking, intonation and inflection during the public reading of the Scriptures is not only commanding but charming. Two maxims to remember: true reading is interpretation; true emphasis is exposition.

It was George Mueller, one of the truly great men of faith and prayer in more recent times, who said: "The vigour of our spiritual life will be in proportion to the place held by the Word in our life and thoughts." Out of his long and fruitful experience he has given six suggestions on "How to read the Bible", and they are briefly presented as follows:

> Read the Scriptures regularly through.
> Read with prayer.
> Read with meditation.
> Read with reference to yourself.
> Read with faith.
> Read in order to carry into practice.

WHAT THE BIBLE DOES

Nehemiah tells us of the wonderful results of the study of the Bible. (1) Sorrow and shame and a sense of sin (v. 9); (2) Salvation and its joys (vv. 10-12); (3) Steadfastness in the commands of God (vv. 14-17); (cf Acts 2:42). Speaking to the students in a large Bible Institute this wise counsel was given: "When reading the Word of God, always remember to prayerfully ask God by His Spirit to interpret what we are about to read, and to make it living in our hearts. Then He will indeed open our eyes to indescribably 'wondrous things' out of the Word of God. We ought to read the Bible to get everything out of it; be careful not to read anything into it, and let nothing remain in it."

Spread the Bible before the Lord; ask Him to reveal to you **your** ignorance and **His** wisdom. Meditation on the Word of God is the chief means of our growth in grace; without this even prayer itself will be little better than an empty form. Meditation nourishes faith, and faith and prayer are the keys which unlock the hidden treasures of the Word. We have great need to be prepared for trials of faith and patience in so great a business as reading the Scriptures with an understanding heart.

Some years ago we were present at a very large conference where a goodly number of gifted brethren were ministering the Word of God. Prior to an afternoon session a young man stood up to read Philippians chapter 2, and, although several addresses were delivered, the effect of the reading on the congregation was profound. It was read in a natural, clear and steady voice, and by one who was obviously at home in the Scriptures.

We ought to inspire our children to read. The right book for the right child at the right time is the proved formula for success. Above all, the early teaching of the importance of reading the Sacred Scriptures will enrich all the future of the child. If necessary, dispose of the television and surround your children with good reading material easily obtained at the library, the church or the Christian book store. Good books can challenge the mind, stimulate the soul and furnish the spirit with encouragement for dark and troublesome times as well as enlighten the eyes of our spiritual understanding.

Dr. Gray, of Moody Bible Institute, Chicago, tells how, after all his college studies, he had never really read and known his English Bible. Attending some convention, he had brought with him a copy of the Epistle to the Ephesians and, going out into the woods, threw himself down on the leafy mould and read and re-read it, until it possessed him, and his soul was aglow with peace and joy. That was how he came to abandon his old cumbrous method of study and take to the simple reading of the Scriptures, letting them speak for themselves and be their own interpreter.

Paul's advice to Timothy was, *"Give attention to reading"* (NKJV), and how important it is today that the reading of the Word of God be continued, for, according to Revelation 1:3, whether read in private or in public we can be assured of the blessing of the Lord.

EIGHT

How to Enjoy the Bible

Too many Christians find the Bible drudgery instead of a delight. Some even say their devotions are deader than the Dead Sea. Yet a man like Jeremiah loved God's Word and left on record this statement, *"Thy words were found, and I did eat them; and Thy Word was unto me the joy and rejoicing of mine heart"* (Jer. 15:16). He found the key to his problem in God's Word. This he ate, *i.e.,* he eagerly appropriated it, and the result was joy and rejoicing in his heart as it can be to all and any who will ask, seek and find. My purpose is to show it should be undertaken by all Christians, both young and old. As we discover its rich treasures, as we dig into the mine of unsearchable treasures, we shall find it to be a most satisfactory portion, and a source of pleasure which never loses its attraction and interest. You have heard of the student who, when asked about his books for study on the Bible, replied, "I haven't any, and, indeed, I don't treat the Bible in that manner; I should not know how!" It will be a hopeful sign for the Christian and the church when there is exhibited the same persistence in Bible study that is shown by the channel swimmers, mountain climbers, Arctic explorers and speed-record breakers. To read, meditate and study the Book of Books will certainly help us to enlarge our borders, expand our capacity and bring development in every way to our own personalities.

MENTALLY

Perhaps the reason why many get so little out of their Bible reading or daily devotions is simply because they are not willing to think. Intellectual laziness lies at the bottom of a large percentage of fruitless Bible reading. People are constantly crying for new methods of Bible study, but what many of them wish is simply some method of Bible study by which they can get all the good out of the Bible without work. We must be willing to work, and work hard, if we wish to dig out the treasures of infinite wisdom and knowledge and blessing which are stored up in the Bible. The conception of the Word of God as a treasure house is a ruling thought of Psalm 119, where we meet such expressions as these:

- *"I have rejoiced in the way of Thy testimonies, as much as in all riches"* (v. 14).
- *"Open Thou mine eyes, that I may behold wondrous things out of Thy law"* (v. 18).
- *"Make me to understand the way of Thy precepts"* (v. 27).
- *"The law of Thy mouth is better unto me than thousands of gold and silver"* (v. 72).
- *"Thou through Thy commandments hast made me wiser than my enemies ... I have more understanding than all my teachers; ... I understand more than the ancients"* (vv. 98-100).
- *"How sweet are Thy words unto my taste"* (v. 103).
- *"The entrance of Thy words giveth light"* (v. 130).
- *"I rejoice in Thy Word, as one that findeth great spoil"* (v. 162).

These are a few specimens only of what the psalmist found in searching the Word of God. All figures are exhausted to describe it—a flood of light and joy; more understanding than all his enemies, teachers or ancient sages; food, both nutritious and delicious; wondrous things, all riches, thousands of gold and silver, great spoil, etc. The whole psalm contains at least fifty such tributes couched in every form of speech.

In the same wonderful psalm, exalting the value and virtue of the Word of God, we learn that a holy life is the highest wisdom and surest defence. The letter can make us knowing, but only the Holy Spirit can make us wise. Wisdom is knowledge put to practical use. Wisdom comes to us through obedience to the commands of God. As a soldier in battle must never lay aside his shield, so we must never leave the Word of God out of our minds; it must ever be with us. To sit at His feet is to be better skilled in divine things than many doctors of divinity. There is more wisdom in the testimony of the Lord than in all the teachings of men if they were all gathered together into one vast library. David said, *"I have more understanding than all my teachers: for Thy testimonies are my meditation"* (Ps. 119:99). He had been taught to observe in heart and life the precepts of the Lord, and this was more than the most venerable sinner had ever learned, more than the philosopher of antiquity had so much as aspired to know. The instruction derived from the Holy Scriptures is useful in so many directions and is superior from many points of view, unrivalled everywhere and in every way. As our soul may make her boast in the Lord, so we may boast in God's Word. *"There is none like it; give it me,"* said David as to Goliath's sword, and so we may say the same as to the Word of the Lord.

The mental horizon widens; it is impossible to live in an intellectual prison if we are in constant contact with this unique library, in which the world's finest poetry, deepest philosophy and noblest literature are found. In Scripture alone do we discover a lucid and trustworthy account of earth's origin and our own descent, a history of our race written from the standpoint of its Creator, a final interpretation of the meaning and glory of life and, above all, a light whose rays illumine the far-flung future, enabling us to peer down into the lake of fire, as well as to look upwards and count the towers of the City of God.

In a sentence, no man can be rightly called well educated if he does not know his Bible, nor called badly educated if he does!

The manners are refined; to breathe the pure air of Holy Writ and to keep company with the holiest and highest of our race necessarily softens our natural roughness and we insensibly adopt the court manners of heaven.

SPIRITUALLY

The Lord Jesus stated a tremendously important principle during His temptation in the wilderness. When the devil suggested that He make bread out of stones to relieve His hunger,

He said, *"Man shall not live by bread alone, but by every word that proceedeth out of the mouth of God"* (Matt. 4:4).

In other words, man's life should not consist simply in eating physical food, such as bread, meat and vegetables. He should also be sustained by spiritual food — *"every word that proceedeth out of the mouth of God."* The Bible is that spiritual food of the believer. Therefore every earnest, conscientious Christian will want to spend a certain portion of each day feeding upon the Scriptures as the bread of God. Just as it is not what we eat that nourishes us, but only what we digest, so it is not what we read that strengthens us spiritually, but only what we assimilate by meditation. When our Lord uttered these words centuries ago He was cutting across all the accepted ideas and standards of His day, and if He were to enter the busy marts and government halls of learning today to repeat His teaching, it would be just as revolutionary. Today the great concern of many nations is food for the physical needs of the ever-expanding population. Yet the Creator of the world and Giver of every good and perfect gift knows that the greatest need of man is the bread of God from heaven. Does frolic, natural food or finance bring peace to the human spirit? Ask the pleasure lover, the gourmet or the miser. You can get along without other books, but to ignore God's Book is to perish. That is why we need the Bible today as a rock for stability, a seed for growth, a sword for defence, and as bread for sustenance and satisfaction. Why is the story of the feeding of the five thousand recorded by each of the four evangelists? Because it sets forth the gift of Christ Himself. The Bible presents Him not merely as a historic character of two millennia ago, but as a real living Person who, having redeemed men by the blood of His cross, now enters into men to be the life-giving principle of their daily lives and still dares to say, *"I am the Bread of Life."* Other miracles exhibited His power and illustrated His work, but this one, in a magnificent way, presents the Person of Christ, the Bread of Life. He is at once historic, universal and personal. Thus the Bible, as the Word of God, feeds and fortifies faith, making it sane and satisfying.

PRACTICALLY

One of the most profitable and enriching methods of studying the Bible is the blessedness of taking either a book at a time, the contents of a chapter or the wonder of a word. Another method is to gather out what is recorded on a particular theme. Such is the fullness of the Word that more than one glorious topic or doctrine can be found in almost every Bible book. Take, as an example, the Epistle of Paul to the Ephesians. It has been fittingly called "The Alps of the New Testament", for here we scale heights and span breadths unknown. What a variety of truth! Think of the captivating, soul-inspiring sketches of the bountiful God, the fullness of Christ and the beneficent Spirit, the resources of the saints, and the utter ruin of the sinner. There is no end of abundance and approach to this epistle. The key phrase is, *"in the heavenlies"* and, as this theme is pursued, what do we find?

- 1:3   We are blessed with Christ in the heavenlies.
- 1:20   Christ has gone up and is enthroned there.
- 2:6   We, too, are seated in Him in the same place.
- 3:10   Heavenly beings there must learn in us the *"many coloured wisdom of God."*
- 6:12   There we meet Satan face to face in our hidden prayer life and on that battlefield we win our victories.

What assurance and peace floods the heart after meditation on such a theme! How helpful we can be to others discouraged by the way as we talk to them about our morning's find and pass on what we have enjoyed. I recall once living for days on the expression, *"blessed with all spiritual blessings"* or *"the benediction of all blessings of His Spirit."* The verse as a whole offers a proof of the three Persons forming the Godhead. A close study of verses 1-14 in Ephesians chapter 1 reveals many of the blessings of the Spirit. To mark these in your Bible and inwardly digest them is to rejoice with joy unspeakable.

1. An unbroken relationship (v. 4).
2. An unquestioned acceptance (v. 6).

3. An unforgettable redemption (v. 7).
4. An unending union (v. 10).
5. An unfading inheritance (v. 11).
6. An unsurpassed seal (v. 13).

In our search of the Scriptures we ought to remember the words of J. A. Bengel: (1) Get everything out of it; (2) Do not read anything into it; (3) Let nothing remain in it. Dr. R. A. Torrey, speaking to his students, said, "When we study the Bible, prayerfully ask the Holy Spirit, every time before we begin to study it, to interpret to us what we are about to read, and to make it a living reality in our hearts, then He will indeed open our eyes to indescribably 'wondrous things' out of the Word of God." If we are not able to take on a whole book, we can always take a chapter and adopt this approach.

1. What is the principal subject of this chapter?
2. What is the leading lesson of this chapter?
3. What is the best verse in this chapter?
4. Who is the principal person of this chapter?
5. What does the chapter teach concerning Christ?
6. Is there, in this chapter, any example for me to follow?
7. Is there, in this chapter, any error for me to avoid?
8. Is there, in this chapter, any duty for me to perform?
9. Is there, in this chapter, any promise for me to claim?
10. Is there, in this chapter, any prayer for me to echo?

(a) Select the chapters you wish to study. Oftentimes it is well to take a whole book (e.g., John) and study the chapters in order.
(b) Read the chapter for today's study five times. Read it at least once aloud.
(c) Divide the chapter into its natural divisions and find headings to describe those divisions in the most impressive way (e.g., See ch. 12 Revelation, Scofield).
(d) Compare the Authorised Version and the Revised Version, or the translations of J. N. Darby, Weymouth, Rotherham and others. Even a liberal translation like

Moffat, or the paraphrase of Phillips enables one to see a text from another point of view.

(e) Write down the leading facts of the chapter in their order.

(f) Make a note of leading personalities in the chapter, and any light thrown on their character.

(g) Note the principle lessons of the chapter. Classify these lessons, e.g., lessons about God, Christ, the Spirit, etc.

(h) The central truth of the chapter.

(i) The key verse of the chapter.

(j) The best verse of the chapter; mark it, memorize it.

(k) Note the verses that are usable for texts for sermons or talks or Bible readings. Make an analysis of the thoughts suggested by these verses.

(l) Study of words and phrases, e.g., John, eternal life.

(m) Write down what new truth you have learned from the chapter.

(n) What definite resolve comes to you as you have studied this chapter—negative or positive.

There are some who, upon reading these words, may say, "We just don't have the time for profitable Bible study." Yet there are ninety-six periods of fifteen minutes in the course of a day. Surely you can give one one-hundredth of your time to this important work that will make all the difference in the world between defeat and victory. Some are well versed in the latest antics of their comic favourites, but they do not grow in the Word of God. Do not misunderstand. We are not saying that one should not read things that bring a smile. We are saying, however, that you are sinning if you allow anything, good or bad, to usurp the place of the Word of God in your life, since this is the great arm that God has given us against temptation.

Why not take even a verse and ask God by His Spirit to reveal its value? Just to meditate on a verse such as John 3:16, "the gospel in miniature", will convince you not only of its systematic summary of truth, but also on its daily sufficiency.

1. The greatest gift: *"God gave His only begotten Son"*.

2. The greatest number: *"The world"*, *"whosoever"*.

3. The greatest blessing: *"Everlasting life"*.
4. The greatest deliverance: *"Might not perish"*.
5. The greatest motive: *"God so loved"*.
6. The greatest security: *"God"*.
7. The greatest simplicity: *"Whosoever believeth"*.

We must learn to wait. Samuel Chadwick says, "Hurry is the death of prayer." You can get more from the Lord in five minutes spent unhurriedly than in thirty-five minutes watching the clock. I am persuaded God knows our heart and He can yield to the obedient, sincere seeker more in a few minutes than many a theologian gets in hours. Several simple rules have helped me in my times with God over His truth.

1. Acknowledge His presence.
2. Breathe out your heart in the expectancy of prayer.
3. Come with a keen desire to concentrate, for *the counsel of the Lord shall stand.*
4. Digest inwardly what God unveils to you.
5. Evangelize, or go out and proclaim what great things God has done for you through the Word becoming flesh.

How blessed to share with others the spoil of Scripture (Mal. 3:16) and prove to a superficial, shallow generation that the greatest thing we can do is to make full use of the Bible, *"for the grass withereth, the flower fadeth; but the Word of our God shall endure forever."* Therefore build your destiny on the immutable, unchanging, inerrant Word of God.

How to Study the Bible

In the study of the Bible it will greatly help us if we continually keep in mind that it is God's Word and comes to us clothed with divine authority. It is not a book primarily for those who think well, but for those who desire to live well. Its truths are not only mental, but also moral. The Word of God has in mind the whole man—body, soul and spirit—and furnishes the diligent student with power for the daily conflict with our three-fold foe, the world, the flesh and the devil. We come to the Bible prayerfully; that refers to the human spirit in communion with God. Meditation on what we read is the function of the soul, the mind. Our obedience to the Word of the Lord is the response of the body, dominated by the spirit, moved by the exercise of the soul. Heart-searching should precede Bible study (Jas. 1:21; 1 Pet. 2:1). Just as many plants will not grow in Africa because the soil is acid, so the truth of God cannot take root in lives made bitter by evil thoughts, purposes and actions. We must come to the Book of God with absolute conviction and confidence that God will surely speak and its message is relevant for the day in which we live. If there are disturbing doubts as to the authority of the Book, let the reader be assured by its claims (2 Tim. 3:16; 2 Pet. 1:21) and by its own authenticating witness (John 6:63; 7:17; Matt. 4:4). In times like these Bible study is absolutely vital for a life of sustained spirituality, effective witness and dynamic love. Bible study is the barometer of the Christian life. Let us look at three simple rules of Bible study.

GUIDANCE

In almost every book of the divine library the opening words are the gateway to a systematic survey and comprehensive outline of the Bible. Many who read these lines will never be able to give themselves to the study of the original languages, Hebrew and Greek.

Yet it is within your power to get a working knowledge of the Bible if you follow basic principles. Find out the precise meaning of the name of the book and, in reverence, pray and with a sanctified heart approach the opening words, claiming God's promise, *"The entrance of Thy words giveth light; it giveth understanding unto the simple"* (Ps. 119:130).

The Bible is the only safe and sure guide by which man can be guided through this changing world. How often we come to a fork in the path to heaven! What should we do? It is wise to ask four questions:

1. Does the Bible give any clear lead as to what should be done?
2. If the circumstances are such that the duty is plain and obvious, though maybe unpleasant, it is most unlikely that God will free us of this burden for another (and perhaps more pleasant) duty.
3. Which way does the cross lie? That was the way Christ chose. It may mean renouncing something or sharing His reproach. Can we smell the scent of the Master's feet?
4. Where does the peace of God lie? "Let the peace of God be umpire in your heart." The psalmist said, *"For Thy name's sake lead me, and guide me"* (Ps. 31:3).

This is ever the design of our Heavenly Father. God guides us by His Word. There must be an unqualified acceptance of the finality and fullness of the Holy Scripts. Where the Scriptures are explicit there is no more to be said. If we refrain from following on, the problem is no longer of guidance but of disobedience. We ought to be crystal clear in our confession. *"I being in the way, the Lord led me."* It was Abraham's servant who said these words. He had certain specific instructions from his Master and a strict adherence to them kept him in the way, and the Lord crowned the mission with success. What confidence to actually know our steps can be ordered in His Word.

GROWTH

The question is rightly asked, to what purpose is our perusal of the Book of Books? We must have a definite objective. If it is only to acquire biblical statistics, our intentions will soon vaporize and vanish. If it is for the glory and honour of God and our own spiritual good, then we shall have the aid of the Spirit of God as a driving force and power within enabling us to continue when tempted to flag or fail.

Our Christian life **starts** through the Word. *"Being born again not of corruptible seed, but of incorruptible, by the Word of God, which liveth and abideth forever"* (1 Pet. 1:23). This seed gets into the very warp and woof of our being and, having been laid hold of by faith, the new life springs up. The soil of our hearts must be free from hindrances, as James warns (1:21), and our spiritual life must take root downward and bear fruit upward. Our Christian life is **sustained** by means of the Word of God. Today we have learned that proper vitamins help to make a balanced diet and to bring health. So the Christian must learn that all spiritual sustenance and strength is to be drawn from the life-giving, nourishing, supernatural Word of God. The Word is essential for the soul and is to be studied for the sake of the soul rather than for sermon making. It is the Book that leads us out to God and to our Lord Jesus Christ in all His majesty, power and glory. Concerning His fullness, none of us will ever fathom it here on earth. All our increasing knowledge of Him as we grow in grace and in knowledge gives but faint glimpses of Him whose name and person is "Wonderful". Our Christian life is **safeguarded** from sin by the Word. *"Thy Word have I hid in mine heart, that I might not sin against Thee"* (Ps. 119:11). In the days of IIis flesh God's Word was the unfailing sword Christ used against the enemy. He is our example and it is imperative that we also have the Word of Christ dwelling in us richly in order that the Holy Spirit may use it for every conflict and crisis.

Our only safeguard and our surest recourse is to the words *"It is written."* Our Christian life is **satisfied** through the Word. Years ago Jeremiah said, *"Thy Word was unto me the joy and rejoicing of mine heart"* (Jer. 15:16). God wants us to be happy people. The truest joy comes in reception, response and reverence for the Bible. Going through this life there are many exceedingly painful sorrows and trials, yet the Word of God can give peace without measure, and joy unspeakable — *"as sorrowful yet always rejoicing."* To know we are safe and Christ is our abiding refuge in view of the coming storm of judgment, why shouldn't we be a joyful people? Was it not Isaiah who wrote that we have something to speak about, something to sing about and something to shout about (Isa. 12:1, 5-6)? Our Christian life can only be **successful** through the Word. Think of the words of Jehovah to Joshua as he is about to enter the Land: *"Thou shalt meditate therein day and night ... for then thou shalt make thy way prosperous, and then thou shalt have good success"* (Josh. 1:8). How vastly different are prosperity and success from God's point of view! These are spiritual Christians who are not rich in this world's goods, yet God's promise is true and we can rest assured that abiding in the center of God's will every need will be met and every blessing will be ours.

GODLINESS

The Bible is distinguished from all other books because it is both living and life-giving. What other book has such a wonderful, winning, witnessing message as this Book of Books? Surely in the midst of the thousands of verses, John 3:16 is most beloved and world-wide in its breadth. The Bible is truly a living Book. In its opening chapters we are told of the breath of life, and the tree of life; and in its closing chapters we again read of the tree of life, also the river of life and the Lamb's book of life. Then, all the way through, its message is of life. God's Word, even today is, *"Choose life"* because of the universal condition of all men: *"Dead in trespasses and sins."*

The Holy Scriptures are God's *"lively oracles"*, given by inspiration of God. If our spiritual life is to be sustained and strong, we must constantly feed on the Word of Life. We must read, mark, learn and inwardly digest the Word, for it is life unto those that find its truth and health to all in a world of disease and death. If our lives are to be effective in prayer and established in doctrine, there must be earnestness of heart. So few Christians seem to be in real earnest. How can we ever be faithful witnesses to the truth, to be able to stand against all the wiles of the devil, and to refute the deceptive arguments of modernism and all those false cults in which the religious world abounds today? We must give ourselves to the meditation of the Scriptures and must diligently adopt some method of systematic study for sobriety, godliness and righteousness. Many today read the Word of God at random, hit-and-miss; in order to pick up some good thoughts for addressing a meeting or giving some help in daily life. This leads to a stunted, scrappy and shallow life. Have a plan. A poor plan is better than no plan at all. The study of the Word leads to a depth of spirituality obtained in no other way. It will give richness and fullness to public service and stability to personal experience.

Let us purpose to hear it (Jas. 1:19); read it (1 Tim. 4:13); study it (2 Tim. 2:15); memorize it (Rev. 1:3); and meditate upon it (Deut. 17:19). It will prove to be the joy and rejoicing of our heart and will make us studious, secure, strong and satisfied (Jer. 15:16).

TEN

MORE PRECIOUS THAN GOLD

The study of the Bible leads to the discovery of ever deepening wonders and undreamed of glories which startle the soul and captivate the spirit plunging it into ecstasies of delight. My heart, my mind, my soul, all that is within me declares it to be so! Did not the Psalmist say, *"More to be desired are they than gold, yea, than much fine gold; sweeter than honey and the honeycomb"* (Ps. 19:10). Someone has also commented, "This is maximum desire and maximum delight!" Moreover God Himself estimates His word as settled (fixed, established, founded forever) in heaven and superior to all other books on earth (Ps. 119:89). Just as the heavens are higher than the earth, so His thoughts, His words, His ways are superior to those of man (Isa. 55:8-9). His word is superior in origin, superior in thought, superior in promise, superior in beauty, superior in purpose, superior in power, and superior in results. We are impressed by its profound simplicity, its inimitable brevity, its unhurried clarity.

THE PERMANENCE OF THE BIBLE

The Bible excites the child, entrances the sage and enriches the student in his highest attainment, the knowledge of God. Year after year it continues to be the best seller. How many read a book one thousand years old? How popular are books on religion? Few books are translated from one language to another that have any sort of circulation. But the Bible is translated into hundreds of languages and dialects, and remains the same imperishable, incorruptible Word of God in every language. God's word alone is sovereign and sufficient. It is true and faithful

(Rev. 21:5) in spite of persecution, destruction, corruption and decay, *"the grass withereth, the flower fadeth: but the word of the Lord shall stand forever"* (Isa. 40:8).

In the world where human things are ever changing and passing away, is there anything durable on which we can depend with certainty? Peter answers in the affirmative (1 Pet. 1:23, 25). To him the Bible was God-breathed, God-given, God-determined and God-durable. He joins Isaiah telling us that the glory of man's achievements fades, the sun, moon and stars shall pass away, but *"the Word of the Lord endureth forever."* It is for us to realize and believe that the Bible does not change with time but that it endures century after century. No one can ever take from your personal experience. You may be confronted with questions which cannot be answered because of lack of Bible knowledge but this one thing is certain, *"Whereas I was blind, now I see"* (John 9:25). The Bible does not need to be defended, you might as well try to defend a lion. No one has to prove the sun shines, the stars twinkle, the moon beams, or the roses have fragrance. The Bible speaks for itself and its life changing results speak forcefully of its heavenly Author. It has changed life for millions of people. It gives peace in place of pain. It translates sorrow into song. This God-breathed book is a **Highway** to heaven and a **Guide** book to God. It is a **Crutch** to the crippled; a **Refuge** to the refugee. It is a **Lamp** to the lost; a **Library** to the learned. It is a **Balm** to the broken-hearted and bereaved; and a **Beacon Light** in the darkness of our age. The daily reading of the Bible is an important part of the destiny of any nation. Not only does the Bible change individuals but nations. The periods of revival and reform go hand in hand in history.

Whenever attention and meditation is focused on in the Bible, new life results spiritually, physically, intellectually and economically. All the need of the church of God, its members, and its ministers has been most fully provided for in the 66 books of the Bible. How could it be otherwise, if we admit the Bible to be the Word of God? Could the mind of God have devised, or His finger sketched an imperfect chart? Impossible. We must either deny the divinity or admit the sufficiency of the Book. We are absolutely shut up to this alternative. Some would argue that things are so totally changed since the Bible was penned, that we need other guidance than that which its precious pages supply. They tell us it ought to be removed from our schools. They tell us society is not what it was; that the human race has progressed; that there has been much development of the power of nature, the resources of science, and the application of philosophy; that to maintain the sufficiency and supremacy of the Bible can only be regarded as childish ignorance and modern stupidity. The men who tell us these things may be very clever and learned. Not for a moment do we prefer ignorance to learning, nor do we despise the advance of science, or treat with contempt discoveries of science or sound philosophy, far from it. We affirm in the words of Christ, "[They] *do err, not knowing the Scriptures, the power of God*" (Matt. 22:29). Men must either deny that the Bible is the Word of God, or admit its sufficiency and supremacy in all ages, and in all countries, in all stages and conditions of the human race. Grant us but this, that God has written a book for man's guidance, and we argue that that book must be amply sufficient for man, no matter when, where, or how we find him. *"All Scripture is given by inspiration of God, that the man of God may be perfect, thoroughly furnished unto all good works"* (2 Tim. 3:16-17). This is enough! To be perfect and thoroughly furnished would make a man independent of all the boasted powers of science and philosophy, falsely so called. The Bible is the answer to all the ills of the whole world. It warns humanity of the sea of sin, of the rocks of ruin, of the pools of passion and of the sandbars of Satan.

In spite of the attacks of little men, the Bible stands like a rock undaunted. Its message has not been corrupted. Its progress has not been curtailed. Its character remains as its Author: eternal, enduring and divine.

ELEVEN

THE PROFIT AND PRACTICAL USE OF THE BIBLE

We should study the Bible for four key reasons. They are: for salvation, for sanctification, for solace and for service. Good reasons, don't you think? Now is the time to get started, for Bible study is vital to spiritual health, whether you are newly converted or a mature Christian. The Bible is truly a Living Book.

This book contains: the mind of God, the state of man, the way of salvation, the doom of unrepentant sinners and the happiness of believers. Its doctrines are holy, its precepts are binding, its histories are true and its decisions are immutable. Read it to be wise, believe it to be safe and practice it to be holy. It contains light to direct you, food to support you and comfort to cheer you. It is the traveller's map, the pilgrim's staff, the pilot's compass, the soldier's sword and the Christian's charter. Here heaven is opened and the gates of hell disclosed. The Psalmist, the prophet Isaiah and our Lord all testify that the Bible will live forever. Thus we are to build our lives, our souls, our hopes, our destiny, on its immutable, unchangeable, inerrant precepts and promises.

The Bible is the only eternal book. It is our greatest national asset, the masterpiece of God. It comes to us drenched in the tears of millions of contritions, worn with the fingers of the saints of all ages, expounded by the greatest intellects and stained with the blood of martyrs. It is the fountain in which dying believers cooled their hot faces, the pillow on which the saints of all ages have rested their heads. It breaks the shackles of the slave, takes heat out of life's fierce fever, the pain out of parting, the sting out of death and the gloom of the grave. The Bible is the old time book, the new time book, the all time book. It will demonstrate its own character and its own power. This is the book of all ages and they who build upon it are as eternal as God. The name of Jesus, the Supreme Personality, the center of the world's desire is on every page in one form or another. Pierce the book anywhere and it bleeds with His precious blood, shed for our redemption. The divine book has all the answers for man's every need. To find them is our greatest privilege and opportunity. J. Edgar Hoover, Director of the Federal Bureau of Investigation, United States Department of Justice, said, "It is quite impossible to believe that progress along the road to righteous living may be accomplished without the guidance of the Bible. It is the source of spiritual food, the solution of life's problems, and the inspiration for Christian living."

Years ago I remember one of our great preachers saying "The Bible is the only visible thing that is eternal" (Mark 13:31) and its Author is always present.

The Bible builds up and gives an inheritance among the sanctified (Acts 20:32). We believe that the Bible, as written in the original Hebrew and Greek languages, is the very word of the only wise and true God. He who saw the end from the beginning, and not only the end, but every stage of the way has made adequate provision for our guidance and instruction for the present and for every moment of our earthly pilgrimage. We therefore hold it to be nothing short of positive blasphemy to assert that we have arrived at a stage in the history of the world in which the Bible is not sufficient for all things pertaining to life and godliness. How vastly different even now our school training is now to those days when we had to memorize: "In Adam's fall, we sinned all, The life to mend, this Book attend." Again: "Praying will make us leave sinning or sinning will make us leave praying." "What we are afraid to speak before men, we should be afraid to think before God."

What a wonderful heritage to be taught and brought up according to the book of God. How can I forget our esteemed and beloved theology teacher leaning over the pulpit and telling us,

The Bible claims for itself that on the original parchments every sentence, word, line, mark, point, penstroke, jot or tittle was placed there in complete agreement with the divine purpose and will. Thus the omnipotent and omniscient God caused the message to be formed as the precise reproduction of His Word. The original text was not only divine as to its origin, but was definitely perfect as to its form.
—L. S. Chafer

Further he warned us that the coming age would be marked by an increasing battle concerning the authenticity and abiding value and virtue of the Word of God. To know the Bible it must be read, meditated upon, and inwardly digested. The farmer does not sow seed today and then sit down and watch a harvest develop tomorrow. We must not expect such a miracle to happen in our Christian service. We must read, reread, pray, compare, enquire, ponder, investigate, wait, pray again. We must testify, set examples, and speak again and again, ever waiting on the Lord, remembering that the husbandman has long patience, but the harvest is sure. The reward has been promised by the Lord of the harvest. *"So shall My Word be that goeth forth out of my mouth: it shall not return unto Me void, but it shall accomplish that which I please, and it shall prosper in the thing whereto I sent it"* (Isa. 55:11).

The Bible is the message of life because it reveals the Living Word and Sovereign Lord who gave His life that we might live. This is the Book which must be translated, published, distributed and read in all languages. It must become practical in all lives over the earth.

TWELVE

The Power of the Bible
HEBREWS 4:12

We believe the Bible comes from God, a divine source, through and by means of the Holy Spirit. In this verse we are shown the sufficiency of His Word. It is striking to note just seven things are said of it:

1. it is the *"Word of God"*
2. it is living, or *"quick"*
3. it is mighty, *"powerful"*
4. it is effectual, *"sharper than any two-edged sword"*
5. it is penetrating, *"piercing"*
6. it is regenerative, *"even to the dividing asunder of soul and spirit"*
7. it is revealing and exposing, bringing to light the *"thoughts and intents of the heart"*

The first book of the Bible was written by Moses; the last book, by the Apostle John. They lived 1,600 years apart and yet they never once contradict each other, but have one and the same message in harmony with all the intervening writers of the 66 books of the Bible. Can you imagine 40 different doctors, physicians and surgeons from seven different countries and speaking different languages writing independently of each other over a period of 1,600 years, compiling a textbook for the treatment of disease? What a mess it would make! Imagine the innumerable superstitions of 1,500 years ago, the blunders of ancient medical practice including spirit incantations and witchcraft all combined in one volume together with the new, ultra-modern scientific methods. How would you like to be treated by a doctor who used that kind of book? You see immediately how absurd the entire thing becomes. But not so with the Bible. It is unique! Moses, writing 1,600 years before the last book of the Bible was recorded, was just as up to date, just as scientific, as Paul or John. This alone is sufficient to establish the supernatural origin and structure, the miraculous nature, and the infallible inspiration of the Bible. *"God, who spake in time past … hath in these last days spoken…"* (Heb. 1:1-2). The story of the Scriptures is the story of your redemption and mine through Jesus Christ. The Scriptures teach the death, burial and resurrection of Christ. Jesus Christ is the gospel! His death, burial and resurrection is the gospel story, and without Him you are lost and doomed. The Bible teaches that there is a hell and a heaven. The way to heaven is by receiving and trusting Jesus Christ. The Bible says, *"All have sinned, and come short of the glory of God"* (Rom. 3:23). The Bible also says *"The soul that sinneth, it shall die"* (Ezek. 18:20). The Bible says the only way to bridge the gap between man and God is through Christ. Jesus said *"I am the way, the truth, and the life: no man cometh unto the Father, but by me"* (John 14:6). Today you can accept the Christ of the Bible, you can know peace of soul, peace of conscience and peace of mind by letting Him come into your heart by faith. The fact that some Bibles are dust collectors is not a joke, even though we often hear stories about it. A little girl told her minister that she had learned everything that was in the Bible. She told the minister, "Sister's boyfriend's picture is in it, Mom's recipe for scones, a lock of my hair from when I was a baby, and a receipt for Dad's watch." We may smile at the child, but the tragedy is obvious. This book says, *"It is appointed unto men once to die, but after this the judgment"* (Heb. 9:27), *"He that covereth his sins shall not prosper"* (Prov. 28:13), *"The wages of sin is death"* (Rom. 6:23), *"Be sure your sin will find you out"* (Num. 32:23), *"Why call ye me, Lord, Lord, and do not the things which I say?"* (Luke 6:46), *"If ye love me, keep my commandments"* (John 14:15), *"For God so loved the world that He gave His only begotten Son; that whosoever believeth in Him should not perish, but have everlasting life"* (John 3:16), *"Whosoever was not found written in the book of life was cast into the lake of fire"* (Rev. 20:15). This is the Word of God, will you accept it? Will you make this your prayer? "I acknowledge that I am a sinner. I believe You died on the Cross for me. The best I know how, I commit myself to you for forgiveness of my sin and for guidance in the future. Amen."

THIRTEEN
THE MAN WHO GAVE US OUR BIBLE

On October 6th, 1536, as the leaves were falling and the winter shadows were lengthening, a little man went out to die in a foreign land. Even his enemies said of him that he was "a learned, good and godly man", yet he was to be put to death by burning at the stake. Today he is remembered with gratitude. Although he is no more, the work which he did will never pass away, for he gave to his fellow-countrymen, for the first time in their own tongue, the Word of God, which lives and abides forever.

On that October day at Vilvoorde, Belgium, his garden, his books and the quiet English charm of the manor house at Little Sodbury seemed a far-off dream. During the years between he had often been, like his Master, a man of sorrows and acquainted with grief. Had it all been worthwhile? Yet the Gloucestershire garden had also known its own peculiar and bitter sorrow. For it was there that he had become impressed with the ignorance about the Bible and the many sad and wicked things that were being done in the name of religion—so much so, that he declared, "If God spares my life, ere many years I will cause a boy that driveth a plough to know more of the Scriptures than thou doest."

God had spared his life, and he had tried to fulfil his vow, but not without danger, difficulty and disappointment. He had applied to the Bishop of London for help in his task and for a place in his service to enable him to have the time to give to his work. But the Bishop had not time for the enthusiasm of the strange little man, and at length he had sorrowfully "understood that there was no room in my Lord of London's palace to

73

translate the New Testament; no, nor yet in all England."

So, in May, 1524, he had sailed to Hamburg, never again to set foot in his native land, but destined to send her a greater blessing than he could ever have bestowed in person. Since then he had been a wanderer, hunted like a deer among the mountains. The foxes had holes, the birds of the air had their nests, but for him there was no place to lay his head in peace.

Then had come the glad day when the first copies of his New Testament had been smuggled into England, where they were carried by a skillfully organized system of colportage into the towns and centers of learning and, almost before the authorities were aware of their presence, they were being openly read, bringing to many joy, comfort and light.

But at last the hunters had run their quarry to earth, and now it seemed, in the shortening days, the end had come: Vilvoorde, the dungeon and the stake. As he had sat in his prison, writing to the governor of the castle and begging for the simplest comforts to lessen the horrors of his lonely cell, he must have been reminded of the day when he had translated a similar letter of the Apostle Paul, in which he asked Timothy for his cloak and his books *but especially the parchments.*

A little time was given him for prayer, and he cried with a loud voice, "Lord, open the King of England's eyes!" The executioner stepped to the stake and tightened the cord around his neck, strangling him. The brushwood heaped about him was set ablaze, and the name of William Tyndale was added to the list of those who have been faithful unto death.

The English Bible is largely the work of William Tyndale. The first words which we learn of the Word of God at our mother's knee we owe to him; the last words of consolation that come to the mind and heart of the dying came first to him. Yet the true greatness of the spirit of man is found in the conviction we have that, if he knew of the blessing of his work he would say, "Not I, but the grace of God that was with me."

FOURTEEN

THE DOCTOR'S BIBLE

W. P. Mackay left home at the age of seventeen to attend college and medical school. His mother was a very godly Christian and, upon his departure, she gave him a Bible, writing her name and his and a verse of Scripture upon the fly leaf. But salvation does not run in the family, and the son had no use for his mother's God or the Bible she had given him. He did not consult its pages, and soon afterwards, while drunk, he pawned it in order to purchase whisky.

His studies at school engrossed him and the Bible was forgotten. Eventually he graduated with high honours and became the head of a large hospital. He also took the lead in an infidel club where they practiced everything that was licentious and vile. He was boldly outspoken in his ridicule of God and the Bible.

The only thing that seemed to give him any thrill at all was when an ambulance would unload a dying victim of an accident, or a patient came under his care whose condition was so critical that the chances of survival were slim. This challenged him to pit his skill against what his colleagues would term the impossible. If the patient pulled through, it only gave Dr. Mackay the opportunity to indulge in vain and inglorious boasting. But God was about to deal with him, bringing the doctor to his senses in a remarkable way.

One day an accident victim was brought to the hospital. The lower part of his body was crushed and horribly mangled. In spite of his condition, on his face was a serene look of peaceful calm, so unusual that it amazed Dr. Mackay, who was accustomed to seeing people suffer.

"What's the diagnosis, doctor?" asked the patient with a

smile. "Oh, I guess we'll pull through," replied Dr. Mackay. "No, doctor, I don't want any guess," the man said. "I want to know if it is life or death. Just lay me down easy anywhere, doctor. I am ready. I am not afraid to die, because my trust is in the precious shed blood of the Lord Jesus Christ, who paid the penalty for my sins at Calvary."

His face radiant with Christian love, he continued, "I know I am going to be with the Lord Jesus Christ if I have to die. But I would like to know the truth; just what is my condition?"

"You have, at the most, three hours to live." Hardened as he was, Dr. Mackay could not but feel sympathy for the dying man. "Is there anything special you would like us to do for you?" he asked.

"Thank you," said the man. "In one of my pockets is a two-weeks pay cheque. I wish you would send it at once to my land-lady, and ask her to send me the book."

"What book is that?" asked the doctor.

"Oh, just the book," the man answered. "She will know."

Dr. Mackay arranged for the man's request to be carried out, and then started on his rounds through the hospital. But those words kept ringing in his ears : "I am ready, doctor. Just lay me down easy anywhere. I am ready."

Dr. Mackay had never been known to inquire about a patient for any personal motive, but for the first time in his life he wanted to know how this one was getting along. He returned to the ward where the injured man had been placed and, seeing the nurse whom he had assigned to the case, he asked her how the man was.

"He died a few minutes ago," the nurse informed him. "Did he get the book?" asked the doctor.

"Yes, it arrived shortly before he died."

"What was it, his bank book?"

"No, it wasn't his bank book," said the nurse. "It's still here, though, if you want to look at it. He died with it under his pillow."

Dr. Mackay went to the bedside, reached under the pillow and pulled out the man's book. It was a Bible. As he picked it up the Bible opened, and the pages turned over to the fly leaf. There was his mother's name and a verse of Scripture. It was the Bible given him by his mother when he had left to attend college—the one he remembered pawning, while drunk, to buy more whisky. He slipped the Bible under his coat, blushing with shame to think that he had despised it so, and rushed upstairs to his private office. There he fell upon his knees and asked God to have mercy upon his soul.

All his life he had known, through the teaching received at his mother's knee, that Christ alone could save and keep. In repentance now he accepted Christ as his own personal Saviour and came into the realization that God was his Father, the Lord Jesus his Saviour and heaven his home.

"For God so loved the world, that He gave His only begotten Son, that whosoever believeth in Him should not perish, but have everlasting life" (John 3:16).

"He that believeth not the Son shall not see life, but the wrath of God abideth on him" (John 3:36).

Have you heeded love's warnings?

THE BIBLE AND CHRISTIAN DISCIPLINE

DEDICATION

This book is dedicated to GEORGE RAINEY
who showed me the way.

CONTENTS

PREFACE

The consideration of the doctrine of discipline has been of great appeal to the writer. Further, there was pointed out in the study of Systematic Theology the great neglect of such a doctrine.

After much exercise of heart and prayer, the conviction was born of God the Holy Spirit to write on the subject of discipline in its application to the Christian life. Thoughts were formulated and preparation made to set forth scripturally the importance of such a theme. In the collection of facts pertaining to the subject, the organization and the securing of the material available, it was discovered that discipline was a field almost wholly untouched in theology. On the other hand, according to the Scriptures and the story of humanity, its message is plain and personal and occupies a preeminent place.

It is, therefore, the purpose of the author to present in permanent record a concise yet comprehensive study of the doctrine of discipline. It is sent forth with no attempt to claim to have the last word on the subject, but rather to clarify its doctrinal import and practical aspect. It is committed to the blessing of Him who is the head over all things to the church.

ONE

THE INTERPRETATION OF THE DOCTRINE OF DISCIPLINE

THE MEANING OF THE WORD

The first essential in the truth of discipline is a proper understanding of its meaning relative to the Christian life. The Oxford Dictionary defines discipline as, "Training; especially of the kind that produces self-control, orderliness, obedience, and capacity for co-operation." In the wisdom-literature of the Bible, the word "discipline" is used in reference to moral discipline and the strenuous cultivation of the righteous life. *"Take fast hold of instruction* [discipline], *let her not go, keep her, for she is thy life"* (Prov. 4:13).

The Hebrew word *musar* translated "discipline," is from the verb *yasar* which Gesenius translates:

1. To chasten or to chastise, to correct, to punish with blows, strokes, Deut. 22:18; 1 Kings 12:11 *"my father chastened you with whips."* Especially of children as corrected by their parents, Prov. 19:18; 29:17; of men chastened of God, Lev. 26:18, 28; Ps. 6:1-2; 38:2.
2. To chastise with words, i.e., to admonish or exhort.
3. The noun form is translated by the words: correction, discipline, instruction and learning.

In the New Testament the example set by the LXX is followed and the LXX translated the Hebrew *musa* by *paideia,* which conveys the thought of training, instructing, education, or discipline. According to 2 Timothy 3:16 (RV), the word for "instruction" is properly rendered "discipline." Moffat sounds the same note in his translation of Titus 2:11-12, *"The grace of God ... schools us to renounce irreligion and worldly passions and to live a life of self-mastery, of integrity, and of piety in this present world."* In the Greek Lexicon of Abbott-Smith, the word *paideia* is translated: (1) the rearing of a child. (2) training, learning, instructing. (3) as in LXX, chastening, discipline. According to the classic Greek the word is rendered "education, mental culture." Immediately something of the great scope of the doctrine is gleaned and the truth pertaining to the life of the believer.

It has been pointed out by H. C. Zabriskie, "God does not discipline one who is not saved, for there would be no purpose in such action. He might judge such a one because of sin, but discipline for Him is always reserved for saved people."[1] God in His wisdom and love administers discipline to His people. It is the badge of sonship and the birthright of all in the family of God. The effective Christian is disciplined in every part of his personality and being—mind, will, body, and spirit. Everyone, all through life's school, needs the correcting hand of discipline. None are exempt from this inexorable law. It is a preparatory school for higher learning. While few care to enroll, nothing teaches better.

> It is a truth, though not the whole of the truth, that life is a school, a process of education. And since this is so, discipline by the Great Teacher, who is infinitely wise and good, is a reasonable accompaniment, although discipline is seldom if ever a desired element from the standpoint of the pupil.[2]

The lessons learned through discipline are never forgotten and become vital factors in the framing of a strong Christian character.

---

1   H. C. Zabriskie, "The Discipline of Grace," *Bibliotheca Sacra* (April-June, 1936) p. 167.

2   Perry W. Sinks, In the Refiner's Fire. (Chicago: Bible Institute Colportage Association, 1911) p. 62.

THE TRUTH RELATIVE TO DISCIPLESHIP

It is interesting to observe that "disciple" and "discipline" are words from the same root. The origin of the word is the Latin *discipulus*, and it is translated "scholar." The root word is found in the Bible only in the Gospels and Acts. It is always used in relation to those who followed the Lord Jesus and learned of Him. The New Testament designates those in the family of God by these words: believers, Christians, saints, brethren, disciples. Thus all the children of God are in the church of God. Such a word as "disciple" implies that the person not only accepts the views of the teacher, but that he is also in practice an adherent. The word has several applications. In the widest sense it refers to those who accept certain teachings, not only in belief, but in life. The disciple of Christ today may be described in the words of Farrar as, "one who believes His doctrine, rests upon His sacrifice, imbibes His spirit, and imitates His example."[3]

A disciple of Christ, then, is a pupil, a learner, a follower, one who sits at Jesus' feet, confesses and obeys Him and lives to do His will. To live such a life is not easy.

Disciples are subject to divine discipline. It is God's curriculum for the construction of character. We cannot learn endurance without hardship. To attain purity of life and lip we must know purging. We cannot be strong without striving. To be a follower of Christ is the way of unselfish sacrificial service and self denial. Those whom God calls to lead others must tread the wine-press alone; they must be made perfect through suffering. The distinctive feature of Christianity is the cross. The test of discipleship is the cross. *"And whosoever doth not bear his cross, and come after me, cannot be my disciple"* (Luke 14:27). The great cost of discipleship is saying no to the desires of self. *"Then said Jesus unto his disciples, If any man will come after me, let him deny himself, and take up his cross and follow me"* (Matt. 16:24). This involves disciplinary measures in our private and personal lives; discipline of the will and its choices; discipline of the mind and tongue; discipline of the whole being of man, spirit, soul, and body. This is discipleship which means discipline. Further, the

---

3   G. H. Trever, <u>International Standard Bible Encyclopaedia</u>, Revised Edition, Volume II. p. 851.

claims of a disciple of Christ must be substantiated not by creeds but by deeds. How searching are the words of Christ to all who would follow Him:

> *If ye continue in my word, then are ye my disciples indeed.*
> *By this shall all men know that ye are my disciples, if ye have love one to another.*
> *Herein is my Father glorified, that ye bear much fruit; so shall ye be my disciples* (John 8;31; 13:35; 15:8).

The manifestation of such a life implies education and a specific course of training. Salvation only becomes effective, either in character or in service, as we lead disciplined lives. The preparatory course of the disciple is often painful and one that necessitates perseverance, yet it is progressive in the realization of the purpose of God. Again, the old question of faith and works is faced. Paul, on the one hand, says, *"By grace are ye saved through faith, and that not of yourselves, it is the gift of God,"* while James, on the other hand, declares, *"Faith without works is dead."* That is not to say good works are the foundation of salvation, but they are the fruit of it. While discipline does not save the Christian, it makes him strong and fitted for the work of Christ and the appointment of every good work. The disciple who does not learn to walk the path of self-discipline often lives to experience the discipline that is divine. On such a path the disciple recognizes the Lordship of Christ; he learns to renounce all for the sake of Christ, and becomes a worthy representative of the One whom he has chosen to follow.

Always, however, no matter how far one might progress in the life of faith, we shall need to lead disciplined lives with respect to the appetites and passions of the flesh. Only as Christ is the center and circumference of our life will we know the secret of peace within and power without. It is to follow the path of Paul, *"I keep under"* the body; to be frank and honest in all relations of life; to be godly through the reading of the Scriptures and the adherence to the quiet hour. To live such a life is to forsake sloth and softness; to renounce worldliness and halfheartedness, for a life of sturdy and consecrated discipline, which magnifies the Lord Jesus Christ.

THE NECESSITY OF DISCIPLINE

In the life of the Christian, discipline is as necessary for the soul as exercise is for the body. The Apostle Peter expressed the same thought when he wrote:

> *That the trial of your faith, being much more precious than of gold that perisheth, though it be tried with fire, might be found unto praise and honour and glory at the appearing of Jesus Christ.* (1 Pet. 1:7)

"If need be." The Lord knows what He is about. The natural man does not like the yoke. Yet Scripture says, *"It is good for a man that he bear the yoke in his youth"* (Lam. 3:27). Why? Because he learns God's lesson in God's way. The Lord makes no mistakes in His dealings with His own. The various testings and trials are not always chastisements, but the disciplining of His children. He desires to draw to Himself and develop through trial the fibers of faith. Often when burdens oppress and affliction crushes, only the present trial is seen instead of the future of God's glorious purpose. The trials of life are only for *"a season"*, and are to be expected in the life of the pilgrim bound for heaven. Though faith is tested now, by and by it will triumph when everything is made manifest at the appearing of Jesus Christ.

Sometimes human suffering is explained as discipline sent upon us in the providence of God. Such a view presents no end of perplexity. It is due to a misunderstanding. Suffering enters the human life and the discipline and blessing that result are not the explanation of the existence of suffering, but a gain from suffering which could not be averted. Discipline is necessary to the strengthening of faith; to the unveiling of the deeper vision and the enlargement of understanding and sympathy in a world of pain.

Thorns and trials, duty and discipline are blessings indeed if they bring the opportunity for the grace of Christ to perfect our character. More and more comes the realization that pain has a noble part in the plan of God for His people, in the maturing of Christian character. The thorny path is made fragrant by the rose of suffering. As the grape must be crushed before the wine flows; as the sycamore tree is bruised before its fruit will ripen; as gold must be put into the fire before it is purified; as the old oak log must be laid on the fire, and flames encircle it, before its imprisoned music is set free, so also is the experience of saints. Yes, it is so. Often we must be laid low before we will look high to the source of all sufficiency. We must know God's smiting before we can appreciate His smiling. The potter must break the vessel before he can make out of the same material a new and beautiful vase. Our hearts must be broken before their richest contents can flow out to a world of bleeding hearts.

Indeed, trials and tribulations, adversities and afflictions are often our biggest benedictions; blessings in disguise; messengers from heaven to discipline our lives in order that in them we might display the excellencies of Christ who has called us out of darkness into His marvelous light. Through such means God purifies, refines, prunes, beautifies, and sanctifies His own, to do His will better and to make us meet for His service. It has been said, "Suffering passes; to have suffered remains." Its gracious after-effect is realized in the words of the writer to the Hebrews, *"Now no chastening for the present seemeth to be joyous, but grievous: nevertheless afterward it yieldeth the peaceable fruit of righteousness unto them which are exercised thereby"* (Heb. 12:11). Thus we learn to have faith during the fires of discipline as aptly expressed in this poem:

> In the furnace of affliction
> It is God who tests the ore;
> Gentle is the hand that leads us,
> Safely home to yonder shore.
>
> In the furnace God does train us,
> Knowing we can stand the test;
> Burns the dross and all that hinders,
> Giving us His very best.
>
> In the furnace does it please Him
> Seeing us in constant pain?
> Nay, through sorrow God is planning,
> Not our ill, but heavenly gain.
> In the furnace do we see Him,

Christ the Lord, who dries our tears?
To His breast He gently folds us,
Lifts us high above our fears.

In the furnace Christ is watching,
With a love that's strong and sure,
Till His own are what He wants them,
Then, sweet home, where all is pure.[4]

How tragic would our lives be if the rod of correction was not administered! How much we owe to the gracious hand of God in our lives in discipline! Without the cross there would be no crown. Without correction there would be no character. Without discipline there would be no devotedness in discipleship. It is an unalterable law and an absolute necessity that in the experiences of the Christian life discipline is imperative. God's plan is not only for our salvation but also for our sanctification. It is through much tribulation that we enter the kingdom of God. It is through discipline that we learn of the dignity of our calling and the duty of the disciple of Christ. Along such a path the Holy Spirit reveals the holy and perfect will of God for our lives.

Discipline is most essential in all relations of life. In the purpose of God it is allowed in the life of the Christian for His glory and the good of the disciplined. It produces fruit and progress in Christian character. To fail in this respect is to live to regret. The lack of discipline in the child of God leads to carelessness of witness, indifference to the claims of Christ and results in a life devoid of fruit to God. While the process of discipline may be most painful, yet to all who have experienced that hand and have been exercised thereby it has been to the enrichment and ennoblement of life.

THE MEANS WHEREBY DISCIPLINE IS EFFECTED

The ways of God are past finding out. How inexhaustible His resources in dealing with the sons of men! Luther says, "God has two rods: one of mercy and goodness, another of anger and

---

4   George Rainey, *Light and Liberty*, Vol. 10, (October 1940), p. 274.

fury."[5] The first rod is for correction, the second rod is for the inflicting of the penalty. In His all-wise, eternal, sovereign counsel He accomplishes His purpose whether in relation to Israel in the Old Testament or in relation to the church in the New Testament. The manner in which His lessons are taught is often by the rod of discipline. The instruments He uses vary.

In the history of Israel God used heathen monarchs to chasten His people. Nations, as do individuals, come under the heavy hand of discipline and the solemn pronouncement, *"Whatsoever a man soweth, that shall he also reap"* (Gal. 6:7). The Lord is slow to anger, but when His anger is kindled even just a little, His wrath is "fierce," that is, very effective.

God used Nebuchadnezzar, king of Babylon, as His rod of affliction on Israel. He was one of the most magnificent figures of ancient history and reigned for forty-three years as a mighty monarch and great builder of an empire. Four times he brought his armies against Jerusalem until the city with its king was subdued and the temple destroyed, making a final end of the kingdom. Yet this calamity was attributed to the Lord. *"The LORD sent against him bands of the Chaldees ... against Judah to destroy it, according to the word of the LORD"* (2 Kgs. 24:2). God, in His sovereign character, is seen as He stretches forth His rod to chastise. The instruments He chooses must obey His will and accomplish His divine purpose.

In the early history of the Christian church God permitted heathen rulers to afflict His redeemed, resulting in the scattering of the truth and the welding together of Christians into a strong, united testimony. Nero's persecution in the first century, the Trajan persecution of the second century, and the Diocletian persecution of the third century were all allowed of God to prosper His cause. It is ever true, "The blood of the martyrs is the seed of the church." In the history of Jacob, God allowed a famine to sweep the land to the working out of His holy design. It is one of the great mysteries of providence that God allows (and even sends) famines, plagues, and wars, as we read in Jeremiah 14:12, *"I will consume them by the sword, and by the famine, and by the pes-*

---

5   A. H. Strong, <u>Systematic Theology</u>, Volume 1. (New York: Charles Scribner and Sons, 1899) p. 351.

tilence." They are facts that none can deny. It is not ours to question or to explain but rather to seek for grace to glorify God in them. The past with its discipline becomes a light to the present in yielding the peaceable fruits of righteousness to the praise and glory of God.

The illness of Job, so painful in its intensity, vindicated the Lord and proved the reality of the faith of Job. The book commences with Job in the process of discipline and concludes with the statement, *"The Lord blessed the latter end of Job more than his beginning"* (Job 42:12). The discipline from the Lord always yields big dividends for it has as its goal the glory of God and the good of the chastened. How good to remember in His methods the ultimate motive!

Again, God's gracious dealings are seen in the history of Naomi and the death of her husband in the land of Moab. Such discipline caused her to leave Moab and to return to Bethlehem to the blessing of the Lord. The God of Abraham, Isaac, and Jacob is the God of the Christian. He is the same yesterday, today, and forever. He still accomplishes His divine pleasure in the lives of His people by His chastisement or by His counsel. *"O the depth of the riches both of the wisdom and knowledge of God! how unsearchable are his judgments, and his ways past finding out"* (Rom. 11:33).

DISCIPLINE ILLUSTRATED
IN THE OLD TESTAMENT

JOB—DISCIPLINE OF SUFFERING

The book of Job occupies a unique place in the volume of God. It possesses a character entirely its own, and teaches lessons which are not to be learned in any other section of inspiration. Of Job, Thomas Carlyle has said:

> I call this Book, apart from all theories about it, one of the grandest things ever written with pen.... A noble Book, all men's book! It is our first, oldest statement of the never-ending problem—man's destiny, and God's way with him here in this earth.... There is nothing written, I think, in the Bible or out of it, of equal literary merit.[6]

The opening pages of this remarkable book present this model patriarch. He is believed to have lived about the time of Abraham, and was the best man who could be found on the earth. There was none other with such a beautiful character. He was perfect and upright, one who feared God and shunned evil. As to possessions and earthly things, they were so abundant that this man was the greatest of all the men of the East. The hand of God had hedged him round about on every side, and his path was strewn with the blessings of the Lord. He had all that heart could wish: children, wealth, honour and prestige from all around. His cup of earthly blessing was full. Yet this mature saint, this successful man was chosen by God to be an

---

6   W. G. Scroggie, <u>Know Your Bible</u>, Volume 1. (London: Pickering & Inglis Limited, 1940) p. 133.

example of suffering, a pattern of endurance. He was subjected to divine discipline not primarily on account of personal sin, but rather for the purpose of proving to Satan the truth of God's estimate of His servant Job.

God, in His grace, had challenged Satan concerning His servant, that there was none like him in all the earth. Satan's retort imputes to Job a sordid motive for his allegiance to Jehovah. Satan claimed that Job loved God not for who God was in Himself, but because of what God had bestowed upon Job personally. For this assertion the Lord allows Satan to attack Job. The great man of the East is thrust into the furnace of affliction, seven times heated for him. Trial after trial comes upon him. In one day all the property of Job was swept away, and all his children died in one dreadful catastrophe. As Job contemplated the wasted fields, the loss of his oxen, asses, sheep, camels, the cold faces of his children and his servants, he bowed his head and cried, *"Naked came I out of my mother's womb, and naked shall I return thither: the LORD gave, and the LORD hath taken away; blessed be the name of the LORD"* (Job 1:21).

Job was no fair-weather saint but faithful and true in his devotion to God. Job acknowledges that God is just as good as He was before, and as much to be praised and loved as ever. In his affliction he is an example of patience and magnifies the name of the Lord. By his words and worship, he proves that his love for God is not founded upon His provisions but His Person. Again God challenges Satan concerning the fidelity of His servant Job. Satan says, *"Skin for skin, yea, all that a man hath will he give for his life. But put forth thine hand now, and touch his bone and his flesh, and he will curse thee to thy face"* (2:4-5). Satan is again allowed to touch Job, this time in his body, and he is smitten with boils from head to feet. His misery is complete! His suffering is acute. The man of prosperity becomes a man of pain and poverty. Then look! The man of esteem and riches, a priest, a ruler, a patriarch, sitting in dust and ashes.

His wife breaks down completely and falling into the devil's snare she urges Job to curse God and die. His three friends, Eliphaz, Bildad, and Zophar, learn of his suffering and come to sympathize. They were miserable comforters and their words were like arrows that added greatly to his pain. Their logic was based on rationalism and thus attributed the suffering of Job to sin. They misjudged him and accused him of sin and their "ministry" was that of condemnation. For every chapter of their messages to Job, he responded with two in return. In these three companions of Job, there is represented the various exercises which engage the consciences of Christians when disciplined. Elihu, another comforter of Job, maintained that the suffering of Job was for the purpose of discipline. Though not far from the truth, he acted as a mediator and presents truth from the viewpoint of God. He shows that it is God's desire to open the understanding of men to truth and right by way of chastening and education.

The outcome is that Job arrives at the end desired of God in all the discipline to which He has been subjecting him. Job, now seeing God, forms a true estimate of himself, and repents in dust and ashes. In the valley of affliction, Job learned his vileness. Through suffering, he beheld the sovereignty of God. In chastening, he learned of his corruption. In trial, he learned the truth of God's kindness and faithfulness to His own. More-over, Satan learned that Job did not serve God for what he could get. Job's wife learned that the loss of the material was not the loss of all. The friends of Job learned that suffering is not always the result of sin. Elihu learned that, even though he thought he was right, and all the others were wrong, the final verdict was in the hands of God. Job now knew that God had allowed him to suffer for His glory and his own personal good. He comes forth from the furnace self-judged, purged, and humbled. Patience had accomplished her noble work. *"Ye have heard of the patience of Job, and have seen the end of the Lord; that the Lord is very pitiful, and of tender mercy"* (Jas. 5:11).

Thus the book of Job furnishes us with further light on the mystery of suffering and pain, and, while it does not solve the problem, it serves to teach us that chastisement is but a test and a revealer of character. It disciplines and educates. The ancients asked: "How can this man be godly if he suffers?" We Christians say: "How can this man be godlike if he knows nothing of suffering?" Many of God's children walk in shrouded paths with broken hearts and bleeding feet. Their diet is the bread of affliction and the water of adversity. They long for the rainbow in the sudden, threatening clouds and wait through sleepless nights for the light that does not come. For such, God unveils His gracious ways with His servant Job.

Though His people are caused to pass through the fire, God in His infinite compassion and tender love watches over His people and works out His divine purposes. God put the story of Job into His imperishable record that it might help other children who walk along similar roads. Job served God out of love to the Lord and was allowed to suffer to vindicate God and to vanquish the devil. May we be counted worthy to suffer for such a cause!

ABRAHAM—DISCIPLINE OF SEPARATION

In the history of Abraham, discipline through separation is exemplified. God called Abraham from the city of Ur in the Chaldees, on the banks of the Euphrates. Archaeologists have uncovered wonderful discoveries there and have shown it to have been a mighty civilization. From a luxurious life, Abraham, at God's command, left all to become a nomad *"dwelling in tents."* The call is described in Acts 7:2-3:

> *The God of glory appeared unto our father Abraham, when he was in Mesopotamia, before he dwelt in Charran, and said unto him, Get thee out of thy country, and from thy kindred, and come into the land which I shall shew thee.*

And in Hebrews 11:8, we read the response of faith. *"By faith Abraham, when he was called to go out into a place which he should after receive for an inheritance, obeyed; and he went out, not knowing whither he went."*

In both the call of Abraham and the choice of Abraham, we learn of the God-planned life. In *Stones of Venice*, Ruskin says, "No man is without a divinely-appointed task, and a divinely bestowed strength adequate for its fulfillment." So it is, in the life of the Christian which begins with the call of God. We are called to real sacrifice even in the separation from all that is dear.

No doubt, if Abraham had not obeyed the voice of God and left the city of his birth, an unmarked tomb would have been his resting place in Ur. Yet the *"friend of God"* lives because of his separation, and God speaks of Himself as the God of Abraham, the God of the faithful. Such a path for the child of God is always paved with the prosperity of the Lord.

Though Abraham left his city, he did not leave behind his kindred nor his father's family. At first, he does not obey completely; his father Terah and his nephew Lot went with him. It is always so difficult to break the ties of nature. In the days of our Lord, He spoke to one man, *"Follow thou me."* His answer was, *"Suffer me first to go and bury my father."* With Terah, Abraham lived for some years on the border of the land to which God had called him. Death finally dissolved this union and Abraham again rises in the energy of faith to pursue his course. Often the follower of Christ is impeded by natural bonds and must learn God's will through self-mortification, which is discipline.

Many have experienced the heavy hand of discipline in the separation from loved ones due to war. Men have been called to renounce the usual routine of life for a life of rigor, sacrifice, separation, and even death for the cause of liberty. The Christian who will live devotedly for God and the cause of Christ must of necessity tread the path of self-denial and separation from the world. This will bring the sneer of the world, but the smile of the Saviour. This will mean discipline to the soul, but will yield the rich deposit of fellowship with Him.

Abraham was tested through famine and he made a sad departure from his God-appointed path. He acted without consulting God and went down into Egypt. There he became inextricably involved in the snares of his own weaving; he was severely censured by an idolatrous king and deported. He had to return to the place of the "Altar" and the "Tent." The Christian life is at a standstill out of the will of God. The road to Egypt always leads to conformity to the world and the collapse of faith. Yet the way back is to move forward into freedom. Abraham learned further how the path of faith is the path of separation in the parting with Lot. His nephew, gratifying his ambition, chooses the well-watered plains, and pitched his tent toward Sodom. Lot walked the path of sight and committed spiritual suicide. Abraham walked by faith and separation to God and was rewarded with the blessing of the Lord.

Abraham is further disciplined in separation from Ishmael. When Abraham was in Egypt, he met Hagar, and she proved to be a thorn in his side for many years. In Genesis 15 God promised Abraham a son. The promise, not being fulfilled immediately, Abraham and Sarah sought to bring it about through Hagar. Such a course resulted in contention, strife, and sorrow. Abraham even prayed to God, *"Oh, that Ishmael might live before thee."* Yet, because he was not the promised seed, he must banish him. Why? The purposes of God did not lie in Ishmael, but in Isaac, the promised seed.

The day Isaac was weaned, Ishmael, the son of Hagar, mocked. He opposed the heir and son (Isaac) and so he must be cast out. This was a great sorrow to Abraham and *"grievous in his sight."* It was hard for Abraham to part with Ishmael. Isaac was to have the sole pre-eminence, and the affections of Abraham must change from Ishmael to Isaac. How slow we are to give Christ His place, and to be able to say, "Not I, but Christ." It is only as the Christian learns to enthrone Christ as Lord of his life that the Holy Spirit will perform His work to glorify God.

Again Abraham walks the path of discipline in his separation from Isaac on the altar of Mount Moriah. This was Abraham's final and greatest test. He had given up Ishmael; now God demands his beloved son Isaac. Abraham is bidden to slay and offer up this child of promise. He does not fail, nor stagger through unbelief, but was fully confident in the faithfulness of God, *"accounting that God was able to raise him up, even from the dead; from whence also he received him in a figure"* (Heb. 19:11, RV). He did also in parable receive him back.

When one is confident that God is almighty as well as faithful, one can obey any word of His without fear. What faith! What self-denial! What discipline of speech, of hopes, of plans is exemplified in the illustrious life of Abraham as he walked the path of faith and separation! What reward and revelation as typified in the "Mount of Provision and Prevision." Abraham is a great pattern of faith and, being disciplined through separation from his country, his nephew, Ishmael, and Isaac, he passed with honours in the school of God.

JACOB—DISCIPLINE OF SURRENDER

The history of Jacob is of peculiar interest to the Christian, for in it is seen the discipline of surrender. It is the conflict of the human will against the divine will of God. Jacob stands out from all others in the Old Testament as a man under a special course of discipline from the Lord. It was necessary to sanctify his will, so that he might do the will of God. The life of Jacob is well appreciated by F. B. Meyer:

> If we can understand the life of Jacob, we can understand the history of the people. The extremes which startle us in them are all in him. Like them, he is the most successful schemer of his times; and, like them, he has that deep spirituality, that far-seeing faith, which are the grandest of all qualities, and make a man capable of the highest culture that a human spirit can receive. Like them, he spends the greatest part of his life in exile, and amid trying conditions of toil and sorrow; and, like them, he is inalienably attached to that dear land, his only hold on which was by the promise of God and the graves of the heroic dead. But Jacob's character was purified by tremendous discipline. The furnace into which he was cast was heated seven times more than it is wont to be heated for ordinary men. Through such discipline his people have been passing for centuries; and surely, before its searching fires, the baser elements of their natures will be expelled, until they recognize the true Joseph of their seed ... towards whom they are being brought.[7]

There were three great periods in the life of Jacob: (1) From his birth to his departure from home; (2) From his departure from home to the land of Laban and what he learned there; (3) His closing days in Egypt, "the end" of the man who was disciplined of God.

---

7   F. B. Meyer, Israel, A Prince with God. (New York: Fleming H. Revell Company, 1933) p. 11.

AT HOME

Though Jacob's life was marked by cupidity and trickery, he valued spiritual things. It was God's purpose that he should possess the right of the firstborn (Gen. 25:23), and He would have it come to pass at His own time, and in His own way. But Jacob could not wait for the fulfillment of God's will and so resorted to his own. He takes advantage of his brother in a weak moment and secures the birthright. What trouble we bring upon ourselves by taking things out of God's hands! Jacob did not behave himself in his father's home. Early on he learned cheating and cunning that marred his character and soiled and spoiled his life. Encouraged by his foolish mother, Jacob launches again a desperate deception to possess the blessing of his aged father. Sin never stops at one act; it is always a chain, one link drawing another. It is like a great explosion that leaves nothing but desolation and ruin behind.

Jacob's sin altered the whole course of his life, and left many sad results. It brought about the hatred of his brother and his flight from home. He found himself a lonely wanderer from the land of promise. It was on the threshold of a new life, after deceit and failure of the old, God met him. His life takes on a new hue and a complete change from this point and in an impressionable and chastened spirit he reaches the land of Laban.

IN THE LAND OF LABAN

God permits Jacob to go into the land of Laban to be further instructed in the divine curriculum. He learned something of patience and its refining character as he awaited the hand and heart of Rachel. He was taught to respect the rights of the first-born, when Leah was given to him instead of Rachel. The truth was brought home to his heart that, *"Whatsoever a man soweth, that shall he also reap."* He was deceived by Laban, cheated out of his wages ten times, and chastened as he saw the machinations of his own flesh in his children. As a shepherd, he watched the flocks by night and day. In the drought and heat of the day, in the cold and frost of the night he learned to care for the sheep. Through the long, tedious hours he was taught of God the lessons of solitude and sympathy.

He learned through sore bereavement that the God of Abraham

and Isaac was his God for refuge and for consolation. Jacob lost his mother, father, Deborah (the old link with the family), Leah and Rachel of his own generation, all of whom were removed by death. Last he was to mourn for his son Joseph. In a scene of sorrow, separation, and death, Jacob found the living God his all-sufficiency. Finally, Jacob came to an end of his service with Laban and sets his face toward Bethel at the command of God. Before he reaches Bethel, he must meet his brother whom he had wronged. He must be changed; his will must be disciplined, for only such a man can be of service to God.

Jacob is left alone by the brook Jabbok. There a man wrestled with him. The man is called *"the angel"* in Hosea 12:4, and it is added, *"even the Lord God of Hosts"* (v. 5), so that we can identify the divine wrestler as the Lord Jesus Christ. Out of the all-night struggle came forth a new Jacob, divinely disciplined in his inner life. No longer the supplanter but a "Prince with God", and as such, he was to have power with men. As the sun rises upon Jacob, he comes into the light with a new name, and a new walk; from carnal Jacob to spiritual Israel. It is only as the child of God reaches Jabbok, the place of pouring out or emptying, that he can claim the blessing of God.

THE CLOSING DAYS OF HIS LIFE

The life of Jacob shows the marks of a disciplined man. At the end of his life he is subdued and useful to and for God. In his lifetime he had made many mistakes, but now he makes no mistakes, for he sees things from God's side. He gathers his feet up into his bed. His earthly walk was over; his pilgrimage was ended. The feet he once controlled have been, through discipline, made subject to God. He digs his own grave (Gen. 50:5). This is always true of a man who learns in the school of God. We must come to this experience, and daily we ought to be digging a bit more of our own graves, if God is to work in and through us to will and do of His good pleasure. As we review this stormy, checkered career we marvel at the operation of the divine will in a human soul.

Out of a man who was a supplanter, a deceiver of his father, bargaining with his brother for his birthright, stealing Esau's blessing, the Master Workman disciplined the life of Jacob until, fully surrendered to God, it became a channel of His grace and blessing. As a servant in a strange land, Jacob learned the path of discipline leads to purging and propriety of soul. As a saint at the brook, Jacob met God face to face, and came to an end of self; pride was laid low; self-seeking was dethroned; ambition was renounced, and he emerges no longer the supplanter, but the sovereign, a prince with God. He is a seer at the end of the trail, he displays the shining glory of this faith as he worships on the top of his staff. What a bright and peaceful close to his distracted, self-willed, God-disciplined life!

How instructive it is to trace the hand of God in our lives and to learn the folly of resorting to our own plans and methods to accomplish God's purposes! How important to find in God a sure resource for all the vicissitudes and ventures and vocations of life!

MOSES—DISCIPLINE OF SELF-RENUNCIATION

It has been well said that greatness is usually forged in the fires of affliction. When God was through with Moses in the Desert University of Sinai, he was a finished product. Greatness comes through debasement. The place at the head of the class in God's School is reached by being the servant of all. Holy decisions and high resolves are always followed by severe testings. So it is in the remarkable record of Moses, the man of God. It is summed up by the Spirit in six verses in God's Book of Martyrs—Hebrews 11:23-28:

> *By faith Moses, when he was born, was hid three months of his parents, because they saw he was a proper child; and were not afraid of the king's commandment. By faith Moses, when he was come to years, refused to be called the son of Pharaoh's daughter; choosing rather to suffer affliction with the people of God, than to enjoy the pleasures of sin for a season; esteeming the reproach of Christ greater riches than the treasures in Egypt: for he had respect unto the recompense of the reward. By faith he forsook Egypt, not fearing the wrath of the king: for he endured, as seeing him who is invisible. Through faith he kept the passover, and*

> *the sprinkling of blood, lest he that destroyed the first born should touch them.*

He was *"mighty"* (Deut. 34:12), and *"very meek"* (Num. 12:3); he was the man who sang the first song (Ex. 15:1); the only man who saw God face to face; the only man whom God buried (Deut. 34:6); the only man for whose body the devil fought (Jude 9); the only man whose name is associated with the last Song, *"the Song of Moses and the Lamb"* (Rev. 15:3). He is a giant of God towering over the sons of men. In such a wonderful person we see the discipline of self-renunciation. The faith manifested by his parents in their defiance of the royal decree is later reproduced in their son. The commencement of one's course gives colour to the whole; and the earliest tuition received in the divine school gives a mold and tone of our character which after years cannot obliterate. The story of Moses is summed up by four special characteristics.

HE REFUSED

His life is characterized by his ability to say no. Though he had been educated in all the wisdom of the Egyptians and was mighty in word and deed, yet he was a master in self-discipline. As son of Pharaoh's daughter, what opportunities he had for pomp, wealth, fame, splendor, and majesty undreamt of in Israel's day. Yet he calculated all carefully and definitely, and then wholeheartedly refused it all. The magnitude of his own renunciation entitled him to lead Israel out of Egypt. How aptly a great writer states his resolve:

> The impulsive ardour of youth will sometimes lead a young heart to say, "This people shall be my people, and their God my God." But there was nothing of that kind here. It was the deliberate resolve of a man who had seen much of life, who knew all that could be urged from every side, and who was come to years. With nothing to gain and all to lose, after thoughtful examination, he descended from the footsteps of the loftiest throne in the world. For a palace there would be a hut; for luxury, hard fare and coarse food; for respect and honour, hatred and

contempt; for the treasures of Egypt, poverty and want; for society of the learned and the elite, association with the ignorant and depraved. But none of these things moved him.[8]

No leader of God's people suffers less than the people he is called to lead. Human leaders rise to place and position in various ways; but God's man can only rise in God's way—through suffering and the disciplining process of life. One must have a firm hold on self before he leads others. Moses knew what it was to deny self. So must all who follow Christ. We are to cease to do evil, then *"learn to do well"* (Isa. 1:16-17). We are exhorted to *"abhor that which is evil,"* then *"cleave to that which is good"* (Rom. 12:9). God takes note of what we "do" as well as what we "do not."[9] This is the path, the self-sacrifice, which the disciple or follower of Christ must pursue. It will cost the disciplining of all our powers. Moses made a great choice and, as a result, his example has survived the centuries. His contemporaries have long been forgotten; the glory of Babylon and Assyria, the wealth and wonders of ancient Egypt are passed away but the influence of Moses is deathless. Why has the memory of Moses been so vividly preserved?

HE CHOSE

He heroically chose suffering and affliction with his brethren. It is one of the first choices recorded in the Bible—"to suffer." He was the forerunner of an innumerable host to follow in its train. The Egyptians were aliens, worshippers of false gods. His people were worshippers of the one true God, Jehovah. How much better to be in poverty and pain with "his brethren" than to be with the heathen princes and aristocrats in the palace of plenty. Their pomp was *"for a season,"* whereas God's pleasures are eternal.

HE ESTEEMED

His choice led to a new course in the purpose of God. Forty years of exile are appointed for him where he was no longer to

---

8   Meyer, <u>Moses, the Servant of God</u>, p. 21.
9   Meyer, <u>Moses, the Servant of God</u>, p. 21.

be a prince but a pupil under the tuition of the Lord. Everyone, from the king on his throne to the maid grinding at the domestic mill, knew what he had done. He kept back nothing, he shunned not to declare his decision. His tongue told it, his face showed it, his actions proved it. His motto was, "No neutrality. If God be God, follow Him; if Baal, follow him." For forty years as a son of Pharaoh's daughter, he was taught the wisdom of men. For forty years as a shepherd and a servant of God, he was taught the wisdom of God. In the common round of the desert, as a shepherd, Moses moves according to the will of God. What lessons are learned in the patient waiting for God's time in the carrying out of His purpose!

HE ENDURED

Moses had the twin graces of patience and perseverance. He endured the refusal of "his brethren"; he endured the coldness of the daughters of Jethro, who left him standing at the well; he endured the opposition of Pharaoh; he endured the long years in the seclusion of Midian; he endured the murmuring of Israel in the wilderness; he endured the idolatry of the nation with whom he was associated; throughout the forty years in the *"waste howling wilderness,"* he endured, the only way that any one shall ever endure—"by seeing Him who cannot be seen."

For forty years he learned to master self as a prince in the royal court. Yet this was not enough, thus the pupil must learn in the school of God's appointment. For forty years he was exiled in the desert of Midian because he had attempted to carry out in his own strength and in his own way the purpose of God for his life. For forty years he had been tending the flock and learning how to use the rod, and all that he learned from God in that period, he must use for the people of God. The rod in his hand for protection becomes the rod of power. He learned the lesson of the bosom. Moses had learned what he had in his hand; now he learns what he has in his heart. He was taught the surety of the divine "Thus saith the Lord" in the judgment of God on Egypt, on Miriam, on the sons of Korah, and on the nations round about. Even in death he experienced the heavy hand of discipline because of the unadvised expression of his lips in the most sacred service for God.

Thus through this faithful and fruitful life for God, discipline accomplished her noble work.

DAVID—DISCIPLINE OF SELF-CONTROL

The richly gifted son of Jesse represents shepherd, poet, minstrel, soldier, exile, and king. The history of David begins in 1 Samuel and ends in 1 Kings, and is characterized by some very bitter and trying experiences before he reached the place of exaltation. Self-control is one of David's chief traits. Such discipline of self is imperative in the cultivation of Christian character. In the story of David's life, from his education to his exaltation, how greatly he exercised self-control in the face of envy, hatred, revenge, and degradation, whether in the higher stations of life or the lowest. He stood the hard tests, in all but one instance, and of that it is written that he repented bitterly. The great shepherd-monarch of Israel became a great soldier, and the great sinner became a great saint. He was disciplined by God in order that he might be prepared for the appointed place of God. How necessary it is to be disciplined if grace is to confer on us some favoured and high office. The record of David's life is preserved for our instruction and profit.

David's life may be summed up in the number of hard schools he passed through. The School of Nature was David's early teacher. Bethlehem, nestling close to Jerusalem, was his home. The rugged, wild, strong, gaunt moorlands of Judea were his familiar haunt as he watched the flocks. In the midst of such natural beauty and pastoral picturesqueness the *"man after God's own heart"* was taught by the schoolmaster of his youth that which coloured all his later life. Here he became such a skilled musician that his fame reached the royal palace and he was called to perform on the harp at court. As an athlete, he disciplined himself to throw a stone with unerring accuracy. His experience in the "School of the Lion and the Bear," taught him the lessons of fearlessness and faith in God. He learned what it was to exercise self-control as a shepherd in the hills of solitude and emerged disciplined for his God-appointed duty of sovereign of a nation.

In the School of the Royal Court he learned the nobility of love and the scourge of envy. After his great triumph over Goliath of Gath, instead of honour came hatred; instead of esteem, envy came in the heart of King Saul. During his stay in the royal palace, David constantly experienced the pressure of the thorn of jealousy. What painful thoughts when the javelin was cast at him with hellish hate, with the intent to pin him to the wall! How keen the hurt when the renewed soul finds service done for Christ is unsung and unappreciated! To be hated and yet to refuse to hate is godlike and is the product of the life that is divine.

In the School of the Camp, David became an alien from the court and an outlaw from society. Now he is to be disciplined in the sorrows of rejection. Though he feared not the lion or the bear or the giant of the Philistines, the enmity of Saul took hold of his heart strings and forced him to flee like a partridge on the mountains. Yet in the day of rejection he allowed no root of bitterness to spring up in the garden of his soul. In patience he waited on the Lord. During this time, he could have taken the life of his foe, yet love won the victory and grace saved King Saul. Such is ever the act of the soul instructed in the ways of God. David sees in all his sorrows the hand of God and they are enshrined in the Book of Psalms. *"I will praise thee forever, because thou hast done it."* The final School of David is that of the Conqueror.

> We have now reached the completion of the third course or circle of David's eventful life, and the close of that wonderful process of preparation which was necessary to qualify him for that high and glorious position for which he was so early destined and anointed; and we enter on another chapter in his history. The period of his rejection is over, and the new and glorious position which he is to occupy is being prepared for him. That course of education which belonged to him as a fugitive and a sufferer, though rightful heir to the throne, closed at Ziklag, the scene to him of bitter sorrow and retribution, but of wondrous deliverance and restoration; and it is there after having returned from the slaughter of the Amalekites, and having sent presents of the spoil of the *"enemies of the Lord"* to all places where he and his men were wont to resort, that the momentous tidings of the death of him whose throne he was to fill reaches him.[10]

---

10   J. B. Stoney, <u>Discipline in the School of God</u>. (London: G. Morrish) p.210.

After an interval of twenty-one years, disciplined David attained his appointed place. Slow and sacrificial had been the steps by which he climbed to the peak and deep the exercise of his soul. For seven years he waited in the "School of Delayed Fulfillment of Promises," but at last his patience and self-control were rewarded. The tide of prosperity sweeps in upon David and he is blessed in all things spiritual and temporal. He established his headquarters at Jerusalem, the capital of the nation. The Ark was restored to Jerusalem, and David in his zeal for God desires to build a temple of worship, but was bidden to defer it (2 Sam. 7). His kingdom was made strong and by his conquests the borders extended from the Red Sea to the river Orontes, and from the Mediterranean to the Euphrates.

During the time of his success, David sinned in his treatment of Bathsheba and Uriah. His sin was not glossed over, as it might have been in the account of his career. The book of Romans brings out the truth that, though the standing of David was not changed before God, this did not prevent the smiting of God. And in the life of the believer, though we are declared righteous, God does not stop His discipline. In the case of David, his guilt is at last dragged into the light and in deep contrition of heart he pours out his confession as found in Psalm 51. For twelve months the shepherd king secreted his sin, sealed his lips, and refused to confess. Psalm 32 tells how he felt. His bones waxed old through his roaring all the day long. Day and night God's hand was heavy upon him. On account of this sin, David was disciplined in the awful anguish it produced in his soul and the subsequent attitude of his family and the multiplied troubles that came upon him.

The sunset of his life is marked by the gracious fruit of discipline and the precious repose that came from God alone. His life had been full of tumult and trouble, storms and sorrows, passion and prosperity, war and blood. He had been tempted, tried, stricken, erring—yet in the main he was a true-hearted man of God—but he ultimately entered the eternal rest of God.

JONAH—DISCIPLINE OF OBEDIENCE

The book of Jonah has been called "the most beautiful story

ever written in so small a compass." It is the history of a prophet who, because of his disobedience, was disciplined by God. Jonah ministered in the days of Jeroboam II (823-782 B.C.) and was no mere creature of human fancy but a real person. He was commissioned by God to carry His Word to the great city of Nineveh. *"Arise, go to Nineveh, that great city, and cry against it; for their wickedness is come up before me"* (Jon. 1:2).

Jonah did not want to see Nineveh repent; deep down in his heart he believed that if they repented, Jehovah would spare them from divine punishment. As far as he was concerned, destruction was their due so that they would no longer be a menace to Israel. How little did he realize the way of protection for Israel from the Assyrian was to bring them to know God and His holy law! Motivated by such thoughts, Jonah boarded a ship for Tarshish, the opposite direction to Nineveh. The name "Jonah" means "a dove." Like the Psalmist, he wanted to take the wings of a dove, and fly away (Ps. 55:6). In his intense, patriotic zeal for Israel he refused to preach to the Gentiles and set his sail westward from hated Nineveh.

What thoughts must have passed through the mind of Jonah as he drew away from the shores of his native city! The grace of God pursued him, and he was unable to hasten his escape from the windy storm and tempest. It is well that the Lord does not allow His servants to continue in disobedience, but brings them back to the path of duty—sometimes, as in this case, by severe discipline. That Jonah could sleep through the storm reveals his obstinate character. In his sleep he was awakened by the frightened sailors and he admitted to being the cause of the storm. He was willing to pay the price of his disobedience and become the saviour of the ship's crew. Then the sailors cast him overboard into the choppy waters of the sea. The record says that God had prepared a *"great fish"* to discipline the recreant prophet, and God's preparations are always perfect. Sir Robert Anderson says,

> In the providence of God, when Jonah was thrown overboard, one of the huge sea monsters was swimming by, his huge gullet gaping like a submarine cavern, and Jonah went down into it, just as a midge might go down

the throat of a man running against the wind.[11]

In such a strange environment Jonah spent three days and nights. One very successful evangelist used to say that Jonah spent a most profitable semester in "Whale College." Jonah learned that his discipline was direct from God, saying: *"Thou hadst cast me into the deep, in the midst of the seas; and the floods compassed me about: all thy billows and thy waves passed over me"* (2:3). In verse 4 of chapter 2, he further explains the fitting form of this discipline thus: *"I am cast out of thy sight."*

It was a solemn experience for his foolish action and rebellion against the will of God. Deep were the exercises of his soul, as the Scriptures reveal, until he discovers the great truth that *"Salvation is of the LORD"* (v. 9). There was no chance of deliverance from such a hopeless position unless God intervened. It illustrates once more the outstanding truth of the gospel, "Thou must save, and Thou alone." So all who would serve the living God must learn this truth. Being commissioned a second time, he sets his face toward Nineveh to preach to them the message appointed by God.

In the power of God, Jonah preached to the godless Ninevites until the city was robed in sackcloth, the outward evidence of inward sorrow for sin. A mighty cry arose to God, from the king on the throne to the commoner. Evil practices were renounced and an entire city turned to God in confession of its sin. They turned from the evil of their ways and found mercy from the Lord. The mercy of God is here bestowed on the Gentiles as well as the Jews.

What was Jonah's reaction as the messenger of Jehovah? He resented the grace of God bestowed upon that city. How often self intrudes into the work of the servant of God! He built a booth on a hill overlooking the city from the east and waited forty days. He was lonely, disappointed, and angry to realize that after proclaiming judgment, God had shown mercy. He would rather see that city burnt up than have his message discredited. So the Lord purposed, by the sheltering gourd vine, which was destroyed with a worm, to teach him and all other

---

11   R. J. Reid, <u>Reflections on Jonah</u>. p. 10.

112

men that His plans are bigger than Israel and that divine love and grace have no national boundaries.

God spared Nineveh on the ground of sovereign mercy and Jonah learned that this was the prerogative of God. The rebuke of the Lord to Jonah recalls the words of Christ to James and John, who wanted to call down fire from heaven on a Samaritan village: *"Ye know not what manner of spirit ye are of."* As workers for the Lord, often our hearts are hard and our vision of a lost world narrow, because we are disobedient to the voice of duty and discipline. Oh to have a heart of compassion for Christless multitudes, and to rejoice with those in heaven over one sinner who repents.

The doctrine of discipline is confirmed in this record of the lives reviewed. From Genesis through Malachi, God is seen instructing, proving, testing, disciplining His people, with a view to sanctifying their will, so that they might accept and do the will of God. The children of Israel in their wilderness journey are a divine commentary on the subject of discipline. The further consideration of the divine portraits of men named above give added support to the study. Joseph, who was tested and who triumphed beautifully, exemplifies the character of one who was perfected through sufferings. The sons of Korah, Miriam, Gehazi, and many others are vivid illustrations of the heavy hand of discipline. The Scriptures abound in authentic sketches of lives that were instructed in God's unique school of discipline for the fulfillment of His purposes.

Discipline may be accepted in either of two ways: we can recognize it has been appointed for our correction, or we can receive it as an experience common to all men. If we do the latter, we shall miss God's purpose in it. How very important it is to learn that nothing happens by chance in the life of the child of God. Each person whose life is recorded in the Word of God has a personal message to our hearts of the ways of God with His own. How appropriate the words of Scripture as a summary of what has been considered:

> *And what shall I more say? for the time would fail me to tell*
> *of Gideon, and of Barak, and of Samson, and of Jephthae; of*

David also, and Samuel, and of the prophets: who through faith subdued kingdoms, wrought righteousness, obtained promises, stopped the mouths of lions, quenched the violence of fire, escaped the edge of the sword, out of weakness were made strong, waxed valiant in fight, turned to flight the armies of the aliens. Women received their dead raised to life again: and others were tortured, not accepting deliverance; that they might obtain a better resurrection: and others had trial of cruel mockings and scourgings, yea, moreover of bonds and imprisonment: they were stoned, they were sawn asunder, were tempted, were slain with the sword: they wandered about in sheepskins and goatskins; being destitute, afflicted, tormented; (of whom the world was not worthy:) they wandered in deserts, and in mountains, and in dens and caves of the earth. And these all, having obtained a good report through faith, received not the promise: God having provided some better thing for us, that they without us should not be made perfect (Heb. 11:32-40).

THREE
DISCIPLINE ILLUSTRATED
IN THE NEW TESTAMENT

THE LIFE OF CHRIST

The contemplation of the person of Christ yields the richest dividends in life. To think of Him in His holy, harmless, spotless life, His vicarious death and victorious resurrection and exaltation to God's right hand is to cause the Christian to bow and worship.

> "Man of sorrows," what a name
> For the Son of God, who came,
> Ruined sinners to reclaim!
> Hallelujah! what a Saviour![12]

The consideration of His sufferings reveals the Father's heart of love, as well as the hand of God in discipline. The path of Christ was characterized by suffering and sacrifice, blood, sweat and tears, devotion, discipline and duty in the fulfilling of the will of God.

His sufferings are far beyond the concept of mortal man. Only in such revelations as Psalms 22 and 69, Isaiah 53, and others shall we learn something of the inner meaning of the cross, and come to know something of the price paid for the redemption of man by Christ. It cost Him a life of unparalleled sorrow as no other could know. Think of Him, misunderstood, ignored, bowed down beneath the weight and misery of a sin-cursed humanity, alone in the garden, alone before the High Priest, alone in the Praetorium, alone on the Via Dolorosa, alone on the cross, suffering with, as well as for, the sons of men.

---

12   P. P. Bliss, <u>Choice Hymns of the Faith</u>, (Belle Chasse: Truth and Praise, Inc.) p. 130.

It cost Him the untold agonies of Gethsemane, where His soul was made exceeding sorrowful. As to the extent of His sufferings, we know little, but it was in relation to our sins, in anticipation of the cross. We hear Him offering up prayers and supplications with strong crying and tears. Blood falls from His noble brow as sweat, the mark of untold agony. Isaiah speaks of His physical sufferings, *"His visage was so marred more than any man, and His form more than the sons of men"* (Isa. 52:14). Oh the awful anguish and pain of the precious body at the hands of sinful men! How desperate the condition of man as seen in his attitude in crucifying the Lord of glory! How great the sum of suffering as told in Psalm 22. Think of the suffering of Christ at the hand of God as He dealt with sin.

Why did He suffer such supreme pain? Because of the price demanded for the salvation of man. So great was the cost of man's eternal salvation, the eternal Son of God was utterly abandoned by God. *"My God, my God, why hast thou forsaken me?"* In full measure He drained the cup of the wrath of God against sin. His death is the central truth of Christianity and the unveiling of His marvelous love and matchless grace to a race dead in trespasses and in sins.

The Scriptures declare that Christ as a Son *"learned obedience by the things which He suffered"* (Heb. 5:8). *"It became him, for whom are all things, and by whom are all things, in bringing many sons unto glory, to make the captain of their salvation perfect through sufferings"* (Heb. 2:10). Christ goes before his army as Captain to lead. He is the Author of salvation, the life and object of the believer's faith. In all these things He is our leader and shows us the way. He became our salvation in His death, our life in His resurrection, and Author of our faith in His example; for He walked the path of faith on earth so that we might follow His steps. He calls His followers to endure hardness and suffering in view of future reward. "Who follows in His train?" The sufferings and scars of Christ are a call to discipleship, an irresistible call. It is the birthright of the Christian to suffer with, and for, the name of Christ.

The great Apostle longed to know Christ in the power of His resurrection and in the fellowship of His sufferings; even so do the disciples of Christ. The scars are the test of discipleship in a spiritual sense in every sincere Christian. Discipline is the seal of our peace and the pattern of our service. Without discipline there will be no devotion; without the cross, no crown can be expected. All heroic service for Christ is inclusive of suffering. The realization of the cost of our salvation in the broken body and broken heart of Christ on Calvary will motivate the Christian to enroll in the school of discipline through suffering.

If the eternal Son walked such a path, can we, His followers, expect anything less? In the heart of God was a cross and in His gracious dealings with His beloved Son He allowed the alabaster box of His life to be broken that blessing might flow out to a world sunk in sin. In like manner, as partakers of His grace, shall not we who have received the gifts of God submit ourselves to the government of God in His all-wise, gracious dealing realizing "Who best can suffer, best can do"? Though the field of discipline has been very little explored, it has been perfectly exemplified in the life of Christ. As the followers of Christ, it is the heritage of the redeemed to display the precious fruits of lives disciplined under the hand of God.

THE APOSTLE PAUL

The greatest Christian in all the nineteen hundred years since the birth of the church at Pentecost is certainly the Apostle Paul. Though born of Jewish parents, he was brought up in the prominent Grecian city of Tarsus, the greatest university city of those days. At the feet of Gamaliel, who was known as the "Beauty of the Law," Saul of Tarsus was instructed in Jewish law. Religiously, Saul was trained as a Pharisee, and thus he imbibed the Pharisaical hatred toward the followers of Jesus. In the early days of the church, he lived to threaten, persecute, and put to death any Christians that he could reach. It is said that he "made havoc" of the church. It literally means that he rooted up the Christians as a hog roots up a fine garden. But all this was gloriously changed in a moment of time along the Damascus road. Saul, armed with authority from the highest religious dignitary in the land, pursues his way from Jerusalem to Damascus to do his utmost to stamp out the new faith, when suddenly he is arrested by the One whom he persecutes. He hears a voice, *"Saul, Saul, why persecutest thou me? It is hard for thee to kick against the pricks."* Saul discovers, in a moment the One who addresses him is Jesus of Nazareth, the founder and leader of the fanatics he hated. In a flash Saul of Tarsus is transformed completely from a foe of Christianity to become its most ardent and faithful friend and adherent. His soul is captured by Christ and goes forth with the motto of his life, *"For me to live is Christ, and to die is gain."*

The course of training offered by Gamaliel is not sufficient for the perfecting of God's servant as seen in the subsequent life of Paul. Many are acquainted with Paul's experience on the road to Damascus, with his visit from Ananias, but few know of Paul's experience in Arabia. It was necessary discipline in order that he might be ready for the purpose of God. Little is said of those three years save the mention in the Epistle of Galatians, *"Immediately I conferred not with flesh and blood: neither went I up to Jerusalem to them which were apostles before me; but I went to Arabia, and returned again unto Damascus"* (1:16-17). What did he learn? In the quietness of that lonely region, the Holy Spirit of God taught Paul and took him step by step along the path of revelation and the work of progressive sanctification. How different the course of training in the School of God. As Dr. Alexander Whyte so beautifully put it, "Saul went into Arabia with Moses and the Prophets and the Psalms in his knapsack, and returned to Damascus with the Romans and the Ephesians and the Colossians in his mouth and in his heart."[13]

In Arabia God wrought a deep and an abiding work in the soul of Saul. Every servant of God that has ever been used to do a mighty work for God and men, has always been called apart for a season of suffering, solitude, and self-revelation. It is in quietness and solitude that we learn to live and serve.

Not only was Paul trained at the feet of the Master in Arabia, but also along the path of persecution and pain. He was saved, sanctified, and set apart to the service of Christ and set forth by the Holy Spirit to bear the name of Jesus before the Gentiles and

---

13   Alexander Whyte, The Apostle Paul. (London: Oliphant, Anderson and Ferrier, 1903) p. 38.

kings and the children of Israel. The path appointed by God for Paul was not to be one of popularity but of persecution, not of gain but of loss, not of liberty but mostly stripes and imprisonment, self-dying constantly while living. He wore not the garments of glory but the grey garb of a bond-slave, of a despised and rejected Christ. The Jews *"bound themselves under a curse, saying that they would neither eat nor drink, till they had killed Paul"* (Acts 23:12).

Paul traveled no easy road. Driven out of Damascus, stoned until he was left for dead at Lystra, raised up by the power of God, he went on from day to day a companion of pain and suffering. Though assaulted at Iconium, stoned at Lystra, railed upon at Corinth, beaten with stripes at Philippi, bound with chains at Jerusalem, shipwrecked, attacked by beasts, left naked, hungry, and close to death's door, he finally was cast into a dark dungeon at Rome, and triumphing through faith, he received the martyr's crown. Certain classic passages in the Corinthian epistles reveal the scope of his sufferings: 1 Corinthians 4:11-13; 2 Corinthians 11:23-28.

The great Apostle began his course with the light from heaven shining down upon his pathway. He continued his career along the path of testing, trial, tears, and temptation. He concluded his course by saying, *"I have fought a good fight, I have finished my course, I have kept the faith"* (2 Tim. 4:7). The light of heaven still streams upon him, having produced a beauty and a moral grandeur which has never been surpassed except by Christ. Tribulation had worked patience with him; indeed, patience had accomplished its perfect work, for he was *"perfect and entire, wanting nothing"* (Jas. 1:4). How blessedly effective the divine discipline, so that Christ was magnified in his body by life and death.

Let us not be guilty of saying that such a program has no appeal for us. As a follower of Christ, it may mean hardship, ostracism, loneliness, and maybe death. Suffering is allowed in the permissive will of God to develop and discipline for His glory and our good. It is medicine not poison, a surgeon not a slaughterer. The fire consumes the dross, the knife removes the dead parts, the chisel cuts away the unnecessary stone of the statue, the pruner's saw cuts off the dead branches that hinder fruit. Such a portrait of the life of Paul as recorded in the New Testament encourages us to enter joyously into the path of suffering, so that through us God may reveal the greatness of His grace and glory.

THE EARLY CHURCH

Next to the cross of Christ, the church of God is the greatest thing God ever wrought, and it is the nearest and dearest object of His heart. Its birthday was the day of Pentecost. Its consummation is foretold in Ephesians 3:10; 5:27; Revelation 21:9-10. Its history has been one of progress, persecution, perversion of truth, and prosperity. From the great day of Pentecost, when three thousand *"gladly received his word,"* and were *"baptized,"* until the present day, countless multitudes have been added through the new birth. Persecution was bound to come.

In the fourth chapter of the book of Acts we witness the first clash with the authorities. The new wine could only burst the old wineskins. There was no place in the dead formalism of the now effete *"Jews' religion"* (Gal. 1:13-14), for the new and vigorous life revealed in the gospel. Holding to traditionalism then, as now, could only stifle and limit the life and liberty, joy and peace, of salvation through grace. The apostles preached *"through Jesus the resurrection from the dead,"* and not only the actual bodily resurrection of the Lord Himself as a great fact, but through Him for all who believed. Immediately they were challenged by the two High Priests, Annas and Caiaphas, who already had the guilt of the murder of Christ on their consciences. These two sought to suppress the truth, but found their threats futile to men who were willing to die for the truth.

Nebuchadnezzar did not frighten the three young men by his threats, nor did the counselors of Darius frighten Daniel. The Emperor Charles V could not intimidate Luther at the Diet of Worms. The apostles, in the teeth of trial and persecution, showed no resentment or complaint. They rejoiced in their afflictions and considered it an honour to be *"counted worthy to suffer shame for the name of Christ."* In the sovereign purposes of God, the early Christians suffered great persecution in order that the evangel of God might reach the uttermost parts of the earth.

In Acts 5, the disciplining hand of God is seen in the story of Ananias and Sapphira. Their judgment has much the same value as the death of Nadab and Abihu, in the early history of *"the church in the wilderness"* (Lev. 10:1-2). Each was a sudden judgment on hypocrisy; each taught the same lesson, that men must reverence God, that God is not mocked. Sometimes discipline seems harsh, but it is not really so. For judgment so vividly taught has been of untold blessing ever since. Men have learned the fear of the Lord thereby. Such judgment has not always been repeated, hence is evidenced the grace of God.

How much the church of God owes to the discipline of God. In the providence of God the church has been permitted to pass through the fires of affliction for the propagation of the truth, for the correction of evil, for the cutting off of saints living in sin, and the bringing to pass His purposes in life and character.

FOUR

THE IMPORTANCE OF DISCIPLINE
FOR CORRECTION IN THE CHRISTIAN LIFE

How great would be the loss in our lives as believers if the Lord's hand had not disciplined us. How much a child of God owes to the parents in the Lord for the rod of correction. Correction in the family of God is to prevent that which is not to God's glory and to promote that which will magnify His grace. Correction should not be regarded as a strange experience for the followers of Christ. It should be a comfort as well as a mark of true discipleship. The Psalmist found all God's dealings with him to be *"according to thy word."* The Word of God never promises the believer exemption from discipline. The Psalmist confesses that before he was afflicted he went astray (Ps. 119:67); that it was good for him to be afflicted (Ps. 119:71); that it was *"in faithfulness"* that the Lord had afflicted him (Ps. 119:75); and that the result had been good, for he had thereby learned God's statutes and the wisdom of keeping them (Ps. 119:71).

The child of God shares with the man of the world the usual ups and downs of life, "the whips and scorns of time." He does not expect preferential treatment. His crops suffer from blight and drought as do others, his vine and fig trees are sometimes fruitless, and his flocks and herds lose their young. The difference lies not in the treatment he receives, but in the grace given to rejoice in the Lord and to find his support in the Living Word and his stability in the Written Word.

The writer of the epistle to the Hebrews reminds us,

> *My son, despise not thou the chastening of the Lord, nor faint when thou art rebuked of him: for whom the Lord loveth he chasteneth, and scourgeth every son whom he receiveth. If ye endure chastening, God dealeth with you as with sons; for what son is he whom the father chasteneth not?* (Heb. 12:5-7).

The discipline may be direct from the Father's hand, as with King David in the matter of Uriah's wife, and of the numbering of the people. Or it may be through famine, as when Elijah prayed for three and a half years of famine because Israel had turned to idolatry. Or it may be through enemies, as when the king of Judah was carried to Babylon, and his armies slaughtered, because of the broken oath and covenant made with the king of Babylon (Ezek. 17:18).

The purpose of God in discipline is to beautify our lives by separating us from evil, and to cleanse our aims of selfish desires so that the motive of our lives might be to please God, that we may truthfully say, *"It is no longer I who live, but Christ who liveth in me."* Discipline is the heritage of sonship that we might be overcomers in the fight of faith. We learn, according to Hebrews 12, that it is for our profit (v. 10); it is taken as a token of sonship (v. 8); it will yield the peaceable fruits of righteousness (v. 11); it will make us *"partakers of His holiness"* (v. 10) if we receive it and respond correctly. In our spiritual education, it plays a most important and serious part. Stern discipline is needed to heal what is lame in our spiritual walk.

The Lord needs to correct His children often on account of sin, slothfulness, slackness, and the refusal to surrender to His will. To refuse to bend is to be broken. The discipline of God corrects our thinking to be more diligent, to examine and judge ourselves, to form regular habits and cultivate godly ways. For a haphazard kind of life is of little influence for God or for good.

Christians tend to become self-sufficient in times of wealth and health. How easy it is to become careless and carnal in our life before God and the world. To prevent this, God graciously allows the blow to fall. He leads us to Himself the hard way. Under such circumstances we learn our weakness and we turn to His omnipotent strength; we feel our emptiness and find His fullness; our loss leads us to His love; and because we feel our need of Him as never before, we get to know Him as never before. There is a new appreciation of God's promises, and a new vitality in our prayers. Life takes on a new vibrancy and thank God for His heart that planned and His hand that permitted correction for His beneficent purposes. We hold fast to the faith that "God in perfect wisdom, perfect love, is working for the best."

FOR CHASTENING IN THE CHRISTIAN LIFE

In the life of the believer, chastening plays a major part in bringing us into the will of God. A world without suffering would be a world without sympathy, sacrifice, courage, and endurance. Not until we reach the Celestial City will we be able to understand the whys and whens of life. Life's mysteries will then be unveiled and a complete and satisfactory solution to the problem of pain will be given. *"For now we see through a glass, darkly; but then face to face: now I know in part; but then shall I know even as also I am known"* (1 Cor. 13:12). Without doubt, chastisement often comes because of our own folly and sin, but chastisement also comes when we are walking in the will of God. Such a thought is strange, but faith rests on the Word of God knowing the great revealing day will make all these things plain.

Thousands of saints have seen the love and goodness of God behind the sorrows and sufferings of life. Discipline becomes an influence for good or for ill, according to the way it is received. As the maxim states, "The same sun that melts the snow hardens the clay." Often God graciously permits chastisement to unveil the deeper riches of His Word and a fuller understanding of His great purposes. Further, to experience the scourging of the Lord is to be brought to the place of utter abandonment to the will of God and to the recognition of the Lordship of Christ. Through chastisement the life is molded and patterned after Christ and the Christian glories in pain rather than pleasure, sorrow rather than song, chastisement rather than comfort.

It is not a question of whether the chastisement is desired, or welcomed, or even if we see it as wise and good, for it is not natural to regard it so. As a fact of experience, *"No chastening for the present seemeth to be joyous, but grievous."* As a fact, chastening is that which everyone cries out against and prays to be delivered from. It is afterward and not at the present that the gracious fruits of discipline are revealed in the character.

The chastisement of the Christian is like the silver in the refining pot (Prov. 17:3), the gold in the furnace (1 Pet. 1:7). One of the most suggestive pictures of God to be found anywhere is in Malachi 3:3, where He is likened to a Refiner and Purifier of silver. The refiner sits beside the crucible, intently watching the mass of molten metal. His task is complete only when the metal is so pure as to reflect his image, mirror-like, on its clear surface. The gold and silver pass through the fire to be purified and to please the refiner with their purity. Thus God allows us to pass through the furnace of chastening in order that we might be sanctified through suffering; cleansed through chastening; purified through pain; and become a "prepared people for a prepared place."

FOR CONFORMITY TO CHRISTIAN CHARACTER

In the soul of the saint who has profited spiritually by his affliction, there is manifested the fruits of righteousness which are by Jesus Christ to the glory and praise of God. Discipline is vitally important in the cultivation of Christian character. We are builders of characters. Unrealized maybe, but not less surely, there is rising slowly day by day through the years a building. Almost every experience, every contact, every touch of another life upon ours, are stones which we lay in life's walls. The experiences of sorrow, suffering, chastisement, conflict, and trial are designed to form character. Character has been described as the robe in which the inner man arrays himself. Day by day we are weaving a garment that we are going to wear in eternity. Character may also be said to be a collection of habits, and the consequences of those habits. The words are well known:

> We sow a thought and reap a word
> We sow a word and reap an act;
> We sow an act and reap a habit;

We sow a habit and reap a character;
We sow a character and reap a destiny.

The lessons of life may be accepted with a view to their role in forming a godly character. On the other hand, they may be rejected, allowing the circumstances of life to mold us as they will. Real nobility of character often needs some circumstance or experience or ordeal to bring it to light and to cause it to shine. Many of the noblest lessons of life are learned in the school of adversity. God corrects, chastens, trains, and educates for a great purpose.

The earthly parent's discipline trains a boy or girl for circumstances, pursuits, occupations, and professions, all of which terminate after the brief span of life. God trains us for an eternal end, "that we should be partakers of His holiness." Not only to be realized in the life to come, but also in this age His holiness is to be reproduced in life and deed by the power of the Holy Spirit.

Discipline that comes into the life in the form of pain, loss, loneliness, ill health, or similar afflictions, is not to mar but to mend that which is lacking in Christian character. "Sanctified afflictions," said Dr. Dodd, "are spiritual promotions." It has been observed that some birds sing their most beautiful melodies only after their eyes are put out. "There is a great want in those Christians who have never suffered." As the Christian poet has said, "When pain ends gain ends."

The trials and testings of life are permitted by God for the enrichment of character. One of the most important requisites in the development of the character of the Christian is patience. It comes through tribulation. *"And not only so, but we glory in tribulations, knowing that tribulation worketh patience"* (Rom. 5:3). It opens the heart's door for comfort to enter, and the consolation thus received is not only heaven-sent medicine for the wounded spirit of the one afflicted, but becomes a divinely-possessed ointment to heal the wounds of many others. This thought was in the Apostle's mind when he wrote:

> *Blessed be God, even the Father of our Lord Jesus Christ, the*
> *Father of mercies, and the God of all comfort; who comforteth*
> *us in all our tribulations, that we may be able to comfort them*

> *which are in any trouble, by the comfort wherewith we our-*
> *selves are comforted of God.* (2 Cor. 1:3-4).

The path of tribulation was the path Christ walked and was the highway of the apostles and martyrs. As followers of Christ, only as we tread the path of pain shall we be able to add sweetness to another's cup of sorrow. The lessons of our own suffering prepare us for the ministry of sympathy in a world of pain. How magnificent the display of triumph over trial and the revelation of character in the following story:

> One of God's disciplined ones, after being blinded in an accident, was told by his doctor that some sight could be saved in one eye but that the other would have to be removed and a glass eye put in. The patient thought a moment and then said, "All right, Doctor, I consent, but if you do have to put in a glass eye, please put a twinkle in it." Thus is illustrated the faith that overcomes.

The cultivation of Christian character comes not only from communion with the Lord, and the consideration of His precepts, and power, but also from overcoming in the conflicts and circumstances of life. The attainment of this goal is to recognize the transcendent importance of character—that learning **to be** will count of far greater worth than learning **to do**. So we must gaze earnestly on the Lord Jesus, and nurture our spiritual appetites. Then Christian character and perfect conduct will become our highest and noblest objective in life.

FOR CHRISTIAN CONDUCT IN THE CHURCH

The importance of the doctrine of discipline is further seen in its promotion of conduct in the church. The golden candlestick in the tabernacle was appointed by God as a symbol of the church as His witness in the world. *"And thou shalt make a candlestick of pure gold: of beaten work shall the candlestick be made, even its base, and its shaft; its cups, its knops, and its flowers, shall be of one piece with it"* (Ex. 25:31, RV).

The tabernacle had no window; its light came from the lamps of the golden candlestick. The church is placed in this dark world to enlighten it. Similarly, Israel was God's witness among the idolatrous nations. The candlestick was of pure gold, which was gold purified in the crucible by being subjected repeatedly to intense heat. It was not made into the candlestick by being cast into a mold, but was beaten or hammered into one piece. Beating is the parallel to suffering. This points to the sufferings of the cross as the birthplace of the church.

The candlestick seems to point to that deep, mysterious union between the head and the body, Christ and the church. It was thus a type of the church which is His body, and is formed from Christ through suffering. We would naturally want to avoid suffering, but it is those who suffer with Christ who will reign with Him. In the history of the church, the Scriptures set forth the discipline of suffering as essential in the life of the church to develop godly conduct in word and deed.

We learn further that the golden candlestick had seven lamps which were fed by pure oil. The oil was obtained by beating the olive berry. God said to Moses, *"And thou shalt command the children of Israel, that they bring thee pure oil olive beaten for the light, to cause the lamp to burn always"* (Ex. 27:20). The beating lacerated the skin of the olive berry, and out poured its pure golden oil for the light. The oil symbolizes the Holy Spirit who dwells in every believer, and through us shines as Christ's witness in the world. Only as we are broken and contrite shall we yield the pure oil for the light.

The conduct of the church will be characterized further by a walk in the light. *"But if we walk in the light, as he is in the light, we have fellowship one with another, and the blood of Jesus Christ his Son cleanseth us from all sin"* (1 Jn. 1:7). Dr. C. I. Scofield in the Scofield Reference Bible says:

> What it is *"to walk in the light"* is explained by vv. 8-10. *"All things   are made manifest by the light"* (Eph. 5:13). The presence of God brings the consciousness of sin in the nature (v. 8), and sins in the life (vv. 9-10). The blood of Christ is the divine provision for both. To walk in the light is to live in fellowship with

the Father and the Son. Sin interrupts, but confession restores that fellowship. Immediate confession keeps the fellowship unbroken.

Further, the conduct of the church is to be characterized by unity. This was the prayer of the Son of God to the Father in His high-priestly prayer in John 17, *"that they may be one, as we are."* The church at Corinth was sadly lacking in discipline and thus there were divisions and disorders among them, domestic and social difficulties, and certain doctrinal errors. So the apostle with deep emotion and love pleads for the unity and harmony of the Lord's people. In like manner, the church at Philippi had internal trouble and the Holy Spirit through the apostle presents Christ and exhorts them to have such a situation corrected by possessing the mind of Christ. It is ever the design of the Holy Spirit to promote the unity and oneness of the body of Christ. It is brought about in many instances by the rod of correction and by the hand of divine discipline.

God in His infinite wisdom allows the church collectively and individually to pass through suffering, persecution, martyrdom, and discipline in order that her conduct might be more real and vivid and Christlike. May we be able to say with the apostle: *"For our light affliction, which is but for a moment, worketh for us a far more exceeding and eternal weight of glory"* (2 Cor. 4:17). *"For I reckon that the sufferings of this present time are not worthy to be compared with the glory which shall be revealed to us-ward"* (Rom. 8:18, RV).

FOR CHRISTIAN SERVICE

Discipline, again, is essential to Christian service. It is woven into the fabric of the servant of Christ. All God's servants know the value of discipline. It is a school few care to enroll in, yet none teaches better. We are told that steel worth only five dollars, if shaped into horseshoes, is worth ten dollars; if made into needles it is worth three hundred and fifty dollars; if manufactured into pocket knives it is worth three thousand, two hundred and fifty dollars; if beaten into springs for watches the same bar is worth two hundred and fifty thousand dollars. The more it passes through the fire and is hammered and pounded and polished, the more valuable it becomes. Hence, many of the crushing experiences of life further and fulfill the plan of the divine Workman.

God often prepared His great ones in the countryside, in some of the quiet places of the earth, farthest away from the busy haunts of men and nearest to the *"secret place of the Most High."* Moses at Horeb, in the deep holiness of the Lord's presence, learned his most influential and enduring lessons. The shepherd monarch, King David, learned to know God while keeping his father's sheep; Elijah learned on the mountain slopes of Gilead; Ezekiel as a captive along the shores of the river Chebar; John the Baptist in the wilderness of Judea; Paul in Arabia; and John the beloved disciple at Patmos. All these are striking examples of the value and practical importance of being alone with God. All who purpose to be equipped and educated for the ministry must retreat there also. God alone can provide and prepare a true minister.

And when we look at the divine Servant, we find that the time He spent in private was nearly ten times as long as that which He spent in public. He, though perfect in understanding and in will, spent nearly thirty years in the obscurity of a carpenter's house at Nazareth, ere He made His presence in public. And, even when He had entered upon His public career, how oft did He retreat from the gaze of men, to enjoy the sweet and sacred retirement of the divine presence. *"And in the morning, rising up a great while before day, He went out, and departed into a solitary place, and there prayed"* (Mark 1:35).

In the four Gospels we read of the magnetic personality of the Son of God, the Creator of heaven and earth. Wherever He was we read that a great throng accompanied Him, listening to the gracious words He spoke and witnessing His deeds of kindness. Yet in His life of obedience we see Him drawing aside from the crowd and from His own to commune with God. The place of solitude is the place of strength. Early in the morning, ere the sky was flushed with the eastern sun, the Lord of glory was found on bended knees alone and praying. His head was oft wet with the dews and damp of night. There He poured out

His heart to God the Father and breathed in the atmosphere of heaven. The perfect man lived in perfect fellowship and unhindered communion with His Father—God.

The absence of secret training and discipline will, necessarily, leave us barren, superficial and theoretical. One thing is evident, namely, that God in His infinite wisdom stretches forth His hand in disciplinary measures for the formation of character of the true and effective servant of God. Lives of such as David Livingstone of Central Africa, Hudson Taylor of China, William Carey of India, Henry Martyn of Persia, Adoniram Judson of Burma, John G. Paton of the New Hebrides, Samuel Marsden of New Zealand, Robert Murray M'Cheyne of Scotland, David Brainerd of America and unnamed multitudes bear abundant testimony to the preciousness of discipline in their witness for the Lord Jesus Christ. What rich treasures we enjoy today through men like ourselves, because they practiced living in the presence of God! How wonderful to be so honoured by God!

CONCLUSION

The study of this important subject reveals that nothing less than unconditional surrender to the Lord Jesus Christ is a fitting response to His sacrifice at Calvary. The demands of Christ have not changed one iota in this day of luxurious living and easy going Christianity. Soldiers give their lives for patriotic reasons. Communists give their all for political reasons. Christians need to be taught by that old conservative minister of the church of Jerusalem, James, the practical discipline of life. It is a life of self-renunciation and undying allegiance to the Christ of the cross. Or as Henry Martyn expressed it: "Lord, let me have no will of my own nor consider my true happiness as depending in the smallest degree on anything that can befall me outwardly, but as consisting altogether in conformity to Thy will." It has been said that the reason the Scots are such a practical and prosperous race is because every Scotsman used to be brought up with the Book of Proverbs in his vest pocket.

The worth of man's religion is determined by the help it is to him. This is supported by the Scriptures. The Epistles of Paul and John represent the interior, the experimental and spiritual side of Christian life while that of James represents the practical. God makes His mosaics of many different pieces, and the blending of all together makes the perfect whole. There is room for James as well as Paul and Peter and John. Paul is the apostle of faith, John of love, Peter of comfort, but James is the apostle of good works, the apostle of every day living. His language is that of the Sermon on the Mount and deals with Christian reality. Many ask is all suffering necessary? Does affliction, heartbreak, disappointment, sickness, and wrecked affection draw us to God or away from God? In the letter of James we learn that if we understand the real purpose of trial then we can actually rejoice. To smile through the sorrow is the work of faith. To praise God in the midst of pain is the sure proof of an inner work of grace. Spurgeon said, "Christian, don't dishonour your religion by always wearing a brow of care." Can we be joyful in the midst of the tests and trials of life? This is ably answered in James.

CALCULATION

Think of the stirring words of the writer, *"My brethren, count it all joy when ye fall into divers temptations"* (1:2). How can anyone be thrilled with tests or have a song in the midst of bitter sorrow? James, like Milton, goes on to show that who best can suffer, best can do. Life was not easy for the early Christians and so today. When we are battered about, our sure resource is the revelation of God, the Holy Scriptures. He allows these trials to come to us so we might become strong, settled and people of mature Christian character. The Holy Spirit wants us to see things in light of Calvary, the life of Christ and the lives of the first century Christians.

CONFIRMATION

The approval of our faith is by means of trial. The very word "trial" means "a test to find approved". The student in school is tested to find out if he has mastered his subject. God allows testing to prove the genuine character of our faith. So much of our life is a mixture, as the word suggests from the purifying of metal. The metal was placed in the refining pot and heated. As the fire burned, the dross came to the top, where it was skimmed off, leaving only the purified metal. God desires truth in the inward parts. Trial comes to burn away that which is not real and to portray to the world the pure gold of Christian faith. Not only does suffering promote faith but it also promotes patience. This was true in the life of Job (5:11). The word patience speaks of the ability to endure as did Moses. How often in our work for God on the mission field and in privileged lands such as Canada, U.S.A. and England, we have been grieved to note how few stick, stand or steadily follow on in Christian life and practice. One of the greatest needs of our age is the ability to go on despite the obstacles and road-blocks that often beset the Christian race.

COMPLETION

The design of the Spirit of God in the life of the Christian is to bring to fruition the work commenced at conversion. It is a life of growth, maturity and completion on a day by day basis. James tells us, *"Let patience have her perfect work, that ye may be perfect and entire wanting nothing."* The thought expressed by the word "perfect" is spiritual maturity, completeness or adulthood. While no one desires trial or discipline, yet no school teaches better. God allows the bitter things of life to come upon us so that we become full and complete. In this way every trial can be sanctified to our profit and blessing to others in the service of God. The more God allows His child to go through the fire or pass through the waters of affliction, the more the life is prepared to be sanctified and useful in the furtherance of His cause. Thus James teaches us that discipline is an essential part of Christian development, and that without great trials there are no great souls.

The authors of the epistles, in writing about all these things, bow in thanksgiving to God who doeth all things well. Our life is like the dial of a clock. The hands are God's hands passing over and over again—the short hand the hand of discipline, the long hand the hand of mercy. Slowly and surely the hand of discipline must pass, and God speaks at each strike; but over and over passes the hand of mercy, showering down sixty-fold of blessing for each stroke of discipline or trial; and both hands are fastened to one secure point—the great, unchanging heart of God. It makes one realize anew that behind the hand of discipline is the heart of love. To God be all the glory!

BIBLIOGRAPHY

Bliss, P. P. Choice Hymns of the Faith. Belle Chasse: Truth and Praise, Inc. Hymn 130.

Brookes, James H. The Mystery of Suffering. London: Fleming H. Revell Company, 1890.

Chafer, Lewis Sperry. Lecture Notes on Soteriology and Ecclesiology. Dallas: Dallas Theological Seminary (unpublished ms.), 1944.

David. London: Marshall, Morgan and Scott Limited, 1933.

Harrington, Vernon C. The Problem of Human Suffering. Chicago: Fleming H. Revell Company, 1899.

Hodge, Charles. Systematic Theology, Volume 1. New York: Charles Scribner and Company, 1872.

Israel, A Prince With God. New York: Fleming H. Revell Company.

Mackintosh, C. H. Notes on Exodus. New York: Loizeaux Brothers, 1879.

Meyer, F. B. Moses, The Servant of God. New York: Fleming H. Revell Company, 1933.

Redemption Songs. London: Pickering and Inglis. Hymn 89.

Scofield, C. I. The Scofield Reference Bible, new and improved edition. New York: Oxford University Press, 1917.

Scroggie, W. Graham. Know Your Bible, Volume 1. London: Pickering and Inglis Limited, 1940.

Sell, Henry T. <u>Studies of Great Bible Characters</u>. New York: Fleming H. Revell Company, 1923.

Sinks, Perry W. <u>In the Refiner's Fire</u>. Chicago: Bible Institute Colportage Association, 1911.

Stoney, J. B. <u>Discipline in the School of God</u>. London: G. Morrish.

Strong, A. H. <u>Systematic Theology</u>, Volume 1. New York: Charles Scribner and Sons, 1899.

Thayer, J. H. <u>A Greek-English Lexicon of the New Testament</u>, corrected edition. New York: Harper & Brothers, 1889.

Trever, G. H. <u>International Standard Bible Encyclopaedia</u>, Revised Edition II.

Watt, John. <u>Old Testament Characters</u>. New York: Loizeaux Brothers, 1934.

Whyte, Alexander. <u>The Apostle Paul</u>. London: Oliphant, Anderson and Ferrier, 1903.

THE AMEN GOD

DEDICATION

This book is dedicated to my tried, tested and true friends in the noblest work in all the world, the work of God.

CONTENTS

ONE

THE AMEN GOD

During the past decade, it has been a burden of my heart to write a personal testimony concerning the goodness, grace and guidance of God. Now much of my allotted time is spent and a little while remains. The days and the years of my pilgrimage have been short, and not without sorrow. A lifetime of service has been spent in the noblest work in all the world.

My spiritual awakening dates back half a century to an Inter-Varsity Camp in the Muskoka Lake district of Northern Ontario. From there to Bethel Chapel in the city of Brantford, the supreme interest in my life and labour has been the living and the true God.

There is scarcely a spot in Palestine that does not bear some geographical name calling attention to the mercies of God. So in my mission over the fields of grace, I have sought to build an altar, pitch a tent and dig a well as a worshipper, witness and worker in the wisdom and power of the triune God. To have the assurance, the assistance and the amen (faithfulness) of the Lord of the harvest is the guarantee of all who are separated for the work unto which they have been called.

I knew whether serving in Canada, Bermuda, America, Asia or Africa, some would be saved in every tribe, in every tongue, in every people and in every nation. My faith in Christ[1] rests upon the character of God that I proved in conversion. My commission[2] rests in the truth of God so closely linked with the character of God. The Hebrew word for truth is *"emet"*, the first and the last and the middle-most of the Hebrew letters of the alphabet. This implies that truth is first and will be last. It combines all extremes and unites all ends. What confidence the called of

---

1   Matthew 11:28
2   John 15:16

God may have! What a solid foundation for all who build, battle and bear His name! He who created the stars and keeps them on their courses is surely able to chart and make clear the way and work of His servants. This I have proved relative to my sweetheart, my sphere and my service. What Abraham told his trusted servant and the Lord His trained statesman, Moses, can be our pattern today. Jehovah is God of the earth because He is the God of heaven. He chose this small speck of dust to be the stage on which the drama of creation, judgment, redemption and ultimate triumph should be played. Our God is able to guide, guard and bring us safely through to the end, not just in small things, but in everything.

How can I forget the God who does wondrous things? The way of God's wisdom is not easy. It does not come to the foolish or to the lazy. It is attainable, but it demands a deep commitment to the Lord. In my early and later days I was fully persuaded of a higher hand and the wisdom that is from above, whether going to live in Bermuda, seeking to win a bride, or best of all, fulfilling the call of Christ.

Bermuda is blessed greatly in the material and the spiritual. From this island endowed with beauty and bounty came a call to the Emmaus Bible School staff for someone to come and bring the Book. Who wouldn't want to go? However, the key men at Emmaus had commitments, various responsibilities and preaching dates. So it was suggested that I should go as I was footloose, family free and had few preaching plans. Many people wondered how I became a snow-bird heading south, but it was God's timing and I was ready. Now the years have winged by and to this day the fruit remains and the missionary interest has never been higher in links with Africa and the furtherance of the work of Christ. In 1992, the first missionary conference with African and Caribbean Brethren was an impetus in the world-wide outreach of Bermuda assemblies. To God be the glory for all that has been accomplished and is still continuing in the unfinished task of Christian Missions in Many Lands.

For some, the pathway of romance has been anything but smooth-sailing and successful. The story of my first love has been given much publicity in articles in overseas magazines and in tract form by the American Tract Society. How quickly a true love story fades after a quarter of a century. Yet it seems but last week that I walked into a Western Union Office in Manhattan to send a telegram to a London lass asking: "Wilt thou go with this man?" For seven years I had been waiting for the girl of my dreams and now the hour had come. How did it happen?

At the close of World War II, in a crowded cafe in Trafalgar Square, I had given a tract, "Safety, Certainty, and Enjoyment," to a young theatrical student. Later, I learned she had been converted, left the London stage, graduated from an English Bible School and dedicated her life to winning theatrical people to Christ all over the United Kingdom. On returning from a trip to the Middle East in 1952, it was momentous to meet this same lass in Scotland. Needless to say, in our few days together we often marvelled at the gracious timing and tender plans of our El-Shaddai (The Mighty God). Letters began to flow back and forth, and finally this never-to-be-forgotten telegram.

For three long months, I had waited for her answer and wondered. On Thanksgiving Day, while preaching at a conference in Detroit, a telegram came with the words: *"Entreat me not to leave thee, or to return from following after thee: for whither thou goest, I will go; and where thou lodgest, I will lodge: thy people shall be my people, and thy God my God: Where thou diest, will I die, and there will I be buried: the LORD do so to me, and more also, if ought but death part thee and me"* (Ruth 1:16-17). It was signed with that beautiful signature, "Love, Audrey." (How lovely to now have a little granddaughter named Audrey.) It was not very long before we were married and the bonds of matrimony bore rich dividends: Jonathan, born in Jerusalem, and David, in Lusaka, Zambia.

What blessed togetherness, so beautiful, but so brief. After being abroad for eight years, we came home on furlough. Our days were filled with family reunions, travel, telling the good news, reports, camps and conferences. It was time to return to our field of service and Audrey and the children went ahead to be with the grandparents in London. Within a few days of their departure a telegram arrived requesting me to come at once, as Audrey was gravely ill. By the time I reached Epping Forest Hospital, it was too late and they took me to the morgue. How awful to break the news to the boys that their mommy was no longer with us. My stay and staff were the words: *"As for God, His way is perfect"* (2 Sam. 22:31). Afterwards I went to Philadelphia, then Augusta, Georgia to commence a new chapter in a life of dedication under His direction.

There are few joys so deep, so labourious, so enriching as serving as an under-shepherd. In the garden city of Augusta, the years passed quickly as I served and the boys grew. Of course many of the believers prayed that some Miss would become a Mrs. in our cottage behind the chapel. What stories could be told of our service, souls and the Southern saints. One Lord's day, I was brought face-to-face with my teenage sweetheart, Grace McLaren. I affectionately called her "my little African". She had been born in Northern Rhodesia and was one of the first pupils of Sakeji School.

We had first met in Simcoe, Ontario where the McLarens settled on returning from Angola. It was my happy privilege from time-to-time to lead the singing and to speak at the Sunday service. Often my focus at the meeting place was on the oldest daughter. She found "grace" in my eyes and I fell in love up to my neck. On a Sunday evening we had to part as I was going to Dallas as a seminary student and Grace to Brantford as a nurse in training. Before leaving I knew all was in His wise hands and we prayed and said goodbye with a kiss.

Then came the rude awakening. Grace said she had seen enough of old clothes and lack of this and that. When she graduated her desire was to paddle her own canoe. She spoke then as a teenager. Twenty-six years later, as a widow with four children, she was once again brought into my life. In some ways it seems incredible. Yet, we believe that nothing is impossible with God. Our hearts overflowed and the Christians at the chapel rejoiced in the news. We were married in Wheaton and started life together in Bermuda. What a honeymoon! We were once four, now we were eight.

After a year of preparation and the commendation of our assembly, we left for Africa. Along the Kafue Road in Lusaka I had made a decision that if God gave me a willing partner, we would return. In my mind, I thought God had blown apart all my plans, but I lived to see He is able "to make a bridge of our broken hopes and a rainbow of our tears." About all we can say is, *"What hath God wrought!"* (Num. 23:23).

What shall I say as to Africa where my wife had been born? It is a land of anguish and ambitions. Yet the dwellers of this place in the sun seem unable to learn what the African must do for himself. For us it is a land of hope situated in the Valley of Achor ("trouble"). It still reaches out with an open door for all skills, science and those who serve God and man.

Palestine, the land of the Bible, is the designated center of the cosmos. Its disclosure and destiny is noted in the Scripture of Truth as the coming mecca to the metropolis of the world. Having a son born in the city of the Great King gave us a link. We love and pray for the peace of Jerusalem. How it thrilled our souls that because we lived and laboured in the land of the Bible and the land of the Black, we shall meet some whose names are in the Book of Life. It's still true, *"They that be wise shall shine like the brightness of the firmament; and they that turn many to righteousness, as the stars forever and ever"* (Dan. 12:3).

On our return from the field to the Land of Promise, a decision was necessary. To us three doors were open, but with God, just one. What would be best? Should I dwell on the Isles of Rest known as Bermuda, the Southern States where I started for God and His gospel, or the Land of the Maple (Canada) where I was once-born as well as twice-born? In the first two there was a place to live, a good promise of well-being and an open door for service. As to Canada, we knew Ontario was too cold after a life-time in the tropics. We decided to visit the great Northwest with its mild maritime climate.

Under God, we came to the capital of British Columbia. Victoria is a quaint, beautiful city bordered by the sea and the mountains. We would be close to Seattle on the mainland of the United States as well as the mainland of Canada and the city of Vancouver. Though I had passed through British Columbia during my student days, we had neither relatives nor close friends to put out the welcome mat. We were assured, even as Moses, that God would send an angel before us to keep us on track and bring us into a place prepared. As the Good Book says, *"all came to pass."* The weather there is like our name; for days it was rain, rain and more rain.

Since the Lord had helped us find a place to live in Jerusalem, Bermuda, and the Cape, we felt confident our God knew the way as well as the place. A fine Christian real estate agent heard of our need and showed up at our dwelling and offered his help. On a drip, drizzle and drenching morning he took us to a place on James Bay, central to the city. When we saw the heritage type house, we liked it at once and learned some elderly Jewish folk lived on the lower level. Now for the bottom line, "How much?"

We needed $40,000 and we did not have that in ready cash. Then I remembered that several years ago while living in Africa, we received word our Bethel Chapel had been sold and a goodly portion of the money was to be used for commended workers of the assembly. At that time, a letter was enclosed from Dr. Les Bier (after whom I was named) with the sum of $15,000. The good doctor suggested if the money was not urgently needed, it could be put in a trust fund for our old age. This we agreed on and now, after all these years, we were in Canada. A long distance call brought the news the money was there and the next day it would turn over for interest rates. It was necessary for me to go to Toronto. Lo and behold, the account had borne great interest and we lacked only $200 of the required amount for the home. Of course, right there in the bank I exclaimed, "Praise the Lord", and wanted to break out saying, "Great is Thy Faithfulness" to my sovereign God and Father in heaven.

How could anyone doubt this was the Lord's doing. "The Lord will provide." It is a proverb God established to show to all His people that the fountain head of His provision is the cross of the Lord Jesus Christ. No man ever lost anything by giving up something for the gospel of God. He is no man's debtor. The sovereign Lord comes to those who put their trust in Him in a three-fold manner. He provides for all their need according to His riches (the principal) with glory (the interest) by Christ Jesus (the Paymaster) (Phil. 4:19). How blessed to find this verse in a book that sets forth life at its brightest and best. Lord, we thank Thee that Thou alone art God.

Publishers Addition

This section concludes with Les and Grace Rainey moving to Victoria, British Columbia in 1994. In 1998, they moved to White Rock, BC where they lived until 2005. At this time, they relocated to Port Colborne, Ontario to live in a retirement home that could provide the necessary care Grace needed. When her health declined, they went to Phoenix, Arizona to be with family. Grace went to be with the Lord on January 27, 2005.

In March 2005, Les decided he should move to Augusta, Georgia where the temperature was milder and there wasn't any snow like in Canada. Currently, Les lives in a little white house provided by Bethel Bible Chapel in Augusta, GA where he once lived 40 years previously with his two small boys, David and Jonathan, following their mother Audrey's sudden death in England. Les continues to serve the Lord in Bible studies, speaking in area assemblies, encouraging the Lord's people and writing meditations for the Choice Gleanings devotional calendar. This book has been published to encourage the Lord's people to serve the Lord faithfully until He returns. The author seeks to encourage readers that the Lord can provide and will guide if we are willing to submit to His will and guidance in our daily living for Him.

HIS GUIDING HAND
BY AUDREY RAINEY

The curtain descended for the fourth and last time on the afternoon performance. I reached for my coat and made my way out into the busy streets of London's West End. Entering my favourite restaurant, I managed to find a table and was soon enjoying my supper, though feeling quite depressed.

Naturally a happy person, I sometimes had spells like this, and the reason was that life seemed empty. In spite of the enjoyment of my work as an assistant stage manager and prospective actress, life was meaningless—a waste of time. Although just nineteen, I was bored and there was no lasting peace or satisfaction in my heart.

As I sat at the table I could see out of the corner of my eye a man with a large white Stetson hat waiting to be seated, and to my surprise (and interest), the hostess guided him to my table. He was accompanied by three other young men—one dressed in the uniform of the Canadian army, the second in that of the Australian air-force, and the third wore the dark blue uniform of the Royal Netherlands Navy. What a mealtime it transpired to be! For these young men were the happiest and liveliest I had ever met. We were soon laughing and talking together as if we had been friends for years.

I wondered where they were planning to spend the evening and discovered that they were going to a "Youth for Christ" rally. Soon the conversation included such phrases as "Living for the Lord," "Being saved," and other expressions which I had not heard before. Apparently my new friends were not interested in such things as theatre-going and dancing, but they had a deep joy and satisfaction in knowing God in an intimate way through the Lord Jesus Christ, and were seeking to serve Him.

By this time, my depression had taken wings and the owner of the hat, Leslie Rainey, asked for my address. The following week we met again, this time by appointment! He carried a large umbrella and wore rubber overshoes. (Being a Canadian in London, it was best to be prepared.) We strolled through St. James Park, passing the theatre where I had spent so many happy hours. Before long, the conversation turned from things of time to those of eternity and Les began to show me how I could experience the joy and peace which he, himself, had received through knowing Christ Jesus as Saviour and Lord.

Alone in my room that evening, I made the decision that was to transform my whole life. As I knelt at my bedside, I knew that the Lord Jesus was in the room with me and He wanted me to turn my life over to Him. I came to Him as a little child and as He whispered to my heart, I simply said, "Yes, Lord." Have you ever thrown up the blind on a glorious morning in spring and felt your heart bursting with happiness as the sunshine streamed into the darkened room? When Christ came into my life, the sunlight of God streamed into my soul and as the days went by and He became more precious to me, I began to understand God's plan of salvation.

It was then that I realized why I had at times experienced unhappiness and dissatisfaction. It was because I had been living a life that was alienated from God. According to the Bible, every person who is born into this world inherits a sinful nature, and I was no exception. Although unrecognized, it had prevented me from having fellowship with a holy God. Although He was the One who made the world and the human beings upon it, He seemed too remote to be my personal friend.

Wonder of wonders! God in His amazing grace and love sent His Son to earth from the glories of heaven, made in the likeness of sinful flesh. He lived a perfect life and died on a cross. There, He took upon Himself my sin and the sin of all mankind. Although I had known all this mentally, God had opened my eyes to see that it had to be appropriated personally. By a simple act of faith, I surrendered my life to Christ and all the wonderful benefits of His death and resurrection were now mine. God became a living reality—nearer than hands or feet. Prayer and Bible reading became vital, a daily conversation between friends. Life took on new purpose because I now had a goal—the joy of witnessing for my Saviour, and the sure and certain promise of eternal life. Peace and real satisfaction became mine as the Lord began to assume His rightful place in my life—and like Paul, I asked, *"Lord, what wilt Thou have me to do?"* The answer came quickly and after a few months I had even exchanged the bright lights of the theatre for Bible College, there to learn more of God's Word and his will for my life.

In the meantime, Les went back to the United States and Bermuda. Three happy and fruitful years in service for Christ rolled by. My missionary activity was to visit theatres in the British Isles to speak of my lovely Lord to those in the entertainment world. I surely believe that God guides the lives of those whom He has called. In 1952 Les, still a bachelor and on his way back to the States from the Middle East, felt he would like to see me again. We met at a smoky railway station in Glasgow, Scotland, six years after our first meeting, and as he said afterwards, "I looked into her eyes and fell in up to my neck." It was love at first sight, or should I say second sight? And as we both prayed for His will in the matter, the voice of God came to both our hearts in the words of Scripture, and we knew that He had made us for each other. He saw the end from the beginning, and only He knew that a seemingly casual meeting in a crowded restaurant would result in a transformed life, a happy marriage, and a life of "togetherness" in the service of our Saviour.

> I'll bless the hand that guided,
> I'll bless the heart that planned,
> When throned where glory dwelleth,
> In Immanuel's land.

A Letter To Christian Youth

I write as a young man to other young people. I enjoy so much the happy things of life: a hike through the hills, a swim, a skate, a game and all that there is to see and do. Yet, I trust that since you have come to the Lord Jesus, you will seek to live to His glory and for the good of others. I am not asking you to do the impossible, for *"with God all things are possible"* if we only believe (Matt. 19:26). Our Lord not only does the saving, but also the keeping.

CHRIST'S KEEPING POWER

When first I trusted Christ I was worried whether I should be able to continue in the Christian pathway. Blessed be His name, the Saviour is also the Keeper of His people. Day by day, I am kept by the power of God. Christ lives in heaven and *"He is able also to save them to the uttermost that come unto God by Him, seeing He ever liveth to make intercession for them"* (Heb. 7:25).

PLEASURES

You will find, as I did, that there are many pleasures this world offers. You will discover that Satan does much to entice the young convert away from Christ and His preciousness. I will not deny that there are pleasures outside of Christ. Music, dancing and all things in fashion are exciting to most youth. But the things and thrills of this earth are passing and are not satisfying. Was it not the Lord Jesus who said, *"Whosoever drinketh of this water shall thirst again: But whosoever drinketh of the water that I shall give him shall never thirst; but the water that I shall give him shall be in him a well of water springing up into everlasting life"* (John 4:13-14)?

The psalmist said, *"In Thy presence is fullness of joy; at Thy right hand there are pleasures forevermore"* (Ps. 16:11). I have found that Christ does sustain and strengthen the one who trusts in Him. He cheers and comforts not only in the sunshine but also in the shadow, in health and in sickness, in gain and in pain, in prosperity and in adversity. Christ can be depended upon every day of your life.

TRIALS WILL COME

You are starting on a new path that leads to heaven. Press on steadfast and faithful, for *"the path of the just is as the shining light; that shineth more and more unto the perfect day"* (Prov. 4:18). You may experience persecution, but God's smile more than compensates for the world's hatred. You will have to endure testing, but that which is genuine will endure the testing. *"That the trial of your faith, being much more precious than of gold that perisheth, though it be tried with fire, might be found unto praise and honour and glory at the appearing of Jesus Christ"* (1 Pet. 1:7).

THE WORD OF GOD AND PRAYER

Above all I covet that you read your Bible daily and pray often to God. Our Lord would have us to read His Book to *"grow in grace and in the knowledge of our Lord Jesus Christ"* (2 Pet. 3:18). All the way you will prove that He is the *"Friend that sticketh closer than a brother"* (Prov. 18:24). He will never fail you nor forsake you, and He will never forget what you do for Him. He will honour you if you will honour Him; bless you as you walk with Him and guide you safely to the haven of eternal rest.

A PERSONAL TESTIMONY

If only I could tell you what Christ means to me! How He has enriched and ennobled the days of my youth! Truly I can now say life is worthwhile since Jesus came into my heart. I long that you should be radiant Christians and useful to the Lord, ever ready to witness for Him by your words and in your life.

FOUR
SHALOM

While I was living in the land of Israel I was greatly impressed with a word that was on everybody's lips. It was the word "Shalom" which we know as "Peace". The first time I heard the greeting, "Shalom, Shalom", was on the day I disembarked from an Israeli ship at Haifa. How can I forget the musical rhythm of Avenu Shalom Aleichem as the El Al Jumbo Jet bearing the Star of David touched down at Ben Gurion airport? What a meaningful word to welcome loved ones to Israel! On that day it meant a lot to me, and does until this hour. Perhaps that is why I like to give my wife Shalom perfume from Israel. In our home you'll find a beautiful plaque with the word "Shalom" cut out of the stones of the land.

ITS MEANING

What does it mean? I believe it is a word that enshrines hidden depths of meaning and conveys the thoughts of rest, well-being, quiet and prosperity, not only in the realm of the physical, but also in the spiritual. Oftentimes a coin loses its lustre and even its lettering becomes blurred through use, yet the value of the coin remains. So the word "peace" and its meaning may be blurred or vague to many, yet thank God, it still sustains its intrinsic value. How good it is to turn to the Word of God and see what the Scriptures say.

ITS MESSAGE

While the word "peace" is familiar in the land of the Bible it is certainly not experienced or enjoyed there. As a nation, Israel is beleaguered by Arabs on every side, blocked, boycotted and bitterly hated, yet the people struggle on for life and liberty. A stable peace for the peoples of the Middle East is not only a problem for Arabs and Jews, it is also the concern of a world that no longer can risk even a small war.

It is the policy of the Western democracies, the Soviet bloc and the neutralist states to preserve peace in Israel, but the question is how can this peace settlement be achieved? The answer is not with countries, conferences or concessions, but in the Messiah. As long as men's hearts are as they are and nations are alienated from the God of peace, we will know little peace in the heart, home or country. True peace is found in the person of the *Sar Shalom*, the Prince of Peace (Isa. 9:6).

Isaiah's language is beautiful and majestic as he presents the Messiah as a Sign to the nation in chapter seven; as the *Sar Shalom* in chapter nine; as a Shoot out of the Palestinian soil in chapter eleven; as a Stone in chapter twenty-eight; as the Shadow of a great rock in chapter thirty-two; as a Shepherd in chapter forty; as a Servant commissioned to carry out the work of redemption in chapters forty-two to fifty, and especially chapter fifty-three; and in the closing chapters of the book as Sovereign of the Universe. How marvelous the title "The Prince of Peace" in these days of wars and rumors of war. When the Messiah takes up the reins of government, He will be the nation's peace. His government will have no limit to its extent, eternal or universal. His rule is based on the everlasting covenant made with the throne of David. *"Peace on earth among men of good will"* (Luke 2:14) is the promise of the Messiah of Israel.

It is the gift of God without money or merit. It is the prayer of the sons of Aaron, *"The Lord lift up his countenance and give thee peace"* (Num. 6:26). Enshrine him now as your *Sar Shalom*, the greatest Jew that ever lived. This blessed peace can be yours today and forever. You'll find it offered by the Great Shepherd of the sheep, and you will prove: *"Oh, that thou hadst hearkened to my commandments! Then had thy peace been as a river, and thy righteousness as the waves of the sea; Thy seed also, had been as the sand and your children numberless as grains of dust; your name would never die, never be lost out of my land"* (Isa. 48:18-19).

FIVE

JERUSALEM

What city in the world is like Jerusalem?

TODAY

No other city has a history to compare with that of Jerusalem. It is not just another city such as New York, London, Rio, Rome, Hong Kong, or Johannesburg. The greatness of ancient cities such as Athens is their past, but Jerusalem's is its future. No place on earth bears such historic and prophetic significance as the ancient city God chose for His habitation. Some think it is too holy for its own good. Others think it's a city of pieces rather than peace. It is the city of the prophet, priest and King; scribe, scholar, *sabra* and saint; the city of the Temple; the city of David; the city of *Shalom*. It is nearly forty centuries old and its people, who have come from the far corners of the earth, throb with a dynamic go, glow and growth. Whether you think of Meggido, Massada, the Wailing Wall, Moses or the menorah, it is the shrine of the Book. Over the earth Jews, Gentiles, Moslems and Christians love this word, Jerusalem.

God's ancient covenant people, the Hebrews, with their illustrious history of blessing and suffering, are linked forever with the only city God ever called "My City". It is the pulsating center of the nation's religious life. The heart-beat of the true Israelite was regulated there. Their national life revolved around the three pilgrimages each year to celebrate the feasts in the Holy City. Jerusalem was the place God appointed for the worship of His name, and all the synagogues of the world were but off-shoots and branches of that divinely chosen gathering center. It is a sacred city, a city that has dominated the world scene out of all proportion to its size and economic importance. The city with peace in its name, (*Salem-shalom* in modern Hebrew and *salaam* in Arabic means "peace"), the city which symbolizes peace and understanding to three great religions, today represents little peace and the least understanding.

YESTERDAY

Nearly forty centuries old, Jerusalem blends the ancient with the new. History as well as prophecy points to her days of gladness, gloom and glory. From the time of the mysterious Melchizedec 4000 years ago until the momentous events under the monarchy of the Messiah, there is no city that can even approximate Jerusalem for her far-reaching historical significance. The first specific prophecy regarding the city is found in the last book of the Law. It is Deuteronomy chapter 12 and five different themes relate to this city that will appear again and again in the literature of Israel throughout the centuries:

1. Jerusalem is chosen of God, referred to six times in this chapter.
2. It is His habitation,[3] also mentioned in the speech of the first martyr in the New Testament (Acts 7:46).
3. Jerusalem is the place where sacrifices and offerings are to be offered. Jerusalem is the place where tithes are to be brought.
4. Jerusalem is the place where God will put His name (Deut. 12:5, 11, 21).
5. Jerusalem is the place where Israel is promised an experience of joy (Deut. 12:7, 12).

How can I forget our years in the city of the Great King (Ps. 137:5-6)? How can I forget the first sight of the city of Jerusalem from the Mount of Olives at the time of the Passover and the birth of our firstborn son, Jonathan? Again and again the words of the mystic Jew (John) who has given to the world five marvelous books come to mind, *"The great city which spiritually is called Sodom and Egypt, where also our Lord was crucified"*(Rev. 11:8). The historical city of Jerusalem is here identified by that

---

3   Psalms 79:7; 132:13; Jeremiah 10:25

which was the crowning act of her guilt, the crucifixion of "their Lord", the Lord of the slain witness. Can I ever forget my visits to the synagogues and listening to the recital of the Law? How empty seemed the religious duties and devotions of the Sanctuary!

Nevertheless in the midst of the traditions and theology, the decadent and dead orthodoxy, a great light dawned in the person of the Messiah. Close by in that picturesque place called Bethlehem nestling in the Judean hills, God's greatest gift was born. The greatest Jew that ever lived was born of a woman, born under law, to redeem those under law (Gal. 4:4). Often along the way in the Holy city, or among the people, I was questioned concerning my beliefs. My answer was always according to the Torah (first five books of the Bible) and the truth of the Tenach (Hebrew Bible used by the Jews); my theology is based on the grandest utterance concerning the Messiah in the whole Book. *"He was wounded for* [my] *transgressions, He was bruised for* [my] *iniquities; the chastisement of* [my] *peace was upon Him, and with His stripes* [I] *am healed"* (Isa. 53:5). Here is the heart of Christianity; the pearl of all prophecies. Apart from the Messiah and what took place outside the city walls of Jerusalem nineteen hundred years ago, there is no understanding to this chapter. In fact, the very name Isaiah can be freely translated, "Jesus saves". These words embrace the Christ, the cross and the crown, or the Anointed, the anguish, and demand an answer. What will you do? *"What shall I do then with Jesus, who is called Christ?"* (Matt. 27:22). Your answer will determine your destiny!

TOMORROW

The city of Jerusalem has had a wonderful past beyond that of any other city in the world. Its future is to be still more glorious. Three great prophets unite to remind us of the far-reaching influence and importance of Jerusalem. Ezekiel informs us that Jerusalem will be the nerve center of the earth. Isaiah hastens to instruct us that it will be the peace center of the world. It is left to Zechariah to vividly warn us that the city will become the storm center of the world. In brief but breath-taking language, the prophet tells us that Jerusalem will be a cup of trembling or reeling, and a burdensome stone, a city besieged. No part of the Middle East, let alone all the world, will escape the awful tribulation that will come upon the earth. On the central citadel of the earth's surface the cup of God's fury will be poured out and it shall be a time of trouble, *"such as never was since there was a nation"* (Dan. 12:1).

Ultimately, Jerusalem will be the city of splendor and glory. Anyone who believes the Tenach must believe in the glorious future of Jerusalem. If some people now think that perfect peace is in store for Jerusalem and the present restoration of the land will settle forever the future of the land and its people, they are very much mistaken. The divine and infallible Word of God predicts a final invasion of Israel's land by an enemy who will then be broken to pieces. There is a time of unprecedented tribulation in store for the restored people in the glory of all lands, called the time of Jacob's trouble.

After the dark night of sorrow and trial, Jerusalem will become the metropolis of the whole world. A king will reign in righteousness, the King Messiah, and a new government will be set up in the city. It will be the government of heaven, of righteousness and peace. The glory of God will cover the city and it will become a royal diadem in the hand of the Lord and she shall no longer be called "Forsaken or Desolate", but *"Hephzibah"* (my delight is in her) and *"Beulah"* (married). But that glory has never been in the past, nor is it today. How few truly believe what the Psalmist depicted, *"Glorious things are spoken of thee, O city of God. Selah"* (Ps. 87:3). How few believe what Isaiah has recorded, *"the Lord of Hosts has purposed and who shall disannul it? His hand is stretched out, and who shall turn it back?"* (Isa. 14:27). Reader, do you know that hand in consolation or condemnation? How foolish not to believe all that the prophets have written concerning the glorious future as well as the grievous folly of the covenant people and the chosen city. Will your name be recorded when the roll is called in the New Jerusalem?

SIX

FRUITS OF THE SANCTUARY

"And in the morning, rising up a great while before day, he went out, and departed into a solitary place, and there prayed."
Mark 1:35

In the four gospels we read of the magnetic personality of the Son of God, the creator of heaven and earth. Wherever He was we read that a great throng accompanied Him, listening to the gracious words He spoke and witnessing the deeds of kindness He preformed. Yet in His life of obedience we see Him drawing aside from the crowd and from His own to commune with God. Hence, our Lord was often found alone.

THE PLACE OF SOLITUDE

Early in the morning, before the sky was flushed with the eastern sun, the Lord of Glory was found on bended knees, alone with God and praying. The perfect man lived in perfect fellowship and unhindered communion with His Father.

In these days of trial, temptation and sorrow, what a divine privilege it is for the child of God to come to the secluded place for prayer. Here the fainting heart is lifted above the earthly cares and the soul's vision is occupied with the majestic person of our wonderful Lord.

Abraham, the friend of God, called out of heathendom for a great and holy purpose, was found in the place of solitude. He pleaded with God on behalf of a wicked city: *"Wilt thou destroy the righteous with the wicked?"* There might be fifty righteous people, and if the Lord found fifty righteous people in the wicked city He would spare the whole place. Then we find the man in whom all the nations of the earth were to be blessed interceding still further—the Lord met all his petitions. Abraham stopped when he got to ten righteous people. God did not. Are we standing yet before the Lord (Gen. 18:22)?

Are we saying prayers instead of praying? If we are to enter this place of fellowship with the Lord of all the earth, we must be more in the closed room. Jacob knew what it was to be left alone (Gen. 32:24). His family, his servants, and his belongings he had sent on ahead. Then Jacob wrestled with a man. It was an all night struggle, out of which there issued a new Jacob. From carnal Jacob to spiritual Jacob.

Moses, a man mighty *"in words and deeds"* (Acts 7:22), was another who learned of God at the backside of the desert. In the seclusion of that wasteland, God filled His servant who became the emancipator of God's people from the tyranny of Pharaoh. All God's servants knew the fruits of being alone with God: Elijah at Cherith, the place of separation from friends but separation to God, Paul the yielded servant of God in Arabia, and John at Patmos. What rich treasure we enjoy today through men of "like passions as we" because they enjoyed the fruits of solitude. Shall we not then search our ways and turn *"again to the Lord"* (Lam. 3:40)? If we are to pluck the fruit of the sanctuary we must get into the deep and sacred retirement of God's presence.

THE PLACE OF SELF-SURRENDER

To enjoy the fruits of the sanctuary, it is imperative that we get alone with God more than we do, and the result will be that our lives will be more fashioned after the perfect model, the Lord Jesus Christ. He was the Lamb of God's providing. *"He was oppressed, and he was afflicted, yet he opened not his mouth: he is brought as a lamb to the slaughter, and as a sheep before her shearers is dumb, so he openeth not his mouth"* (Isa. 53:7). The self-emptied one was *"obedient unto death, even the death of the cross"* (Phil. 2:8).

It is only as the child of God reaches Jabbok, the place of pouring out or emptying, that we can claim the blessing of God. By the brook of Jabbok our self sufficiency is replaced by God's sufficiency, our self seeking, our pride, our ambition is displaced by the eternal satisfier of our souls. That night by the brook, the Holy Spirit through Hosea tells us Jacob *"wept and made supplication"* (Hos. 12:4). If our intercession is tearless, we will never experience what Jacob did, of being changed from supplanter to sovereign Israel, a prince with God. As a prince with God, he now had power with men. Power with God always precedes power with men.

The following day the sun rose on Jacob. It is only as we realize the fact that we are dead to sin, that sin no longer has dominion over us (Rom. 6:14), as we are alive unto God in Christ Jesus (Rom. 6:11), we shall experience a transformation as Jacob did. The great big "I" so prominent in every one of us is laid aside and by the grace of God we say in the language of the hymn:

> All to Jesus I surrender,
> Lord I give myself to thee,
> Fill me with Thy love and power
> Let Thy blessings fall on me.

THE PLACE OF STRENGTH

How often the joy of our salvation causes our hearts to burn within us; yet at other times our hearts are cold, our spirit reaching almost zero. In this state, we have a full recovery at the throne of grace. There the heart is bowed and we pass from the region of sight to that of realization in the presence of God. This must be our stronghold in the day of testing and lukewarmness, with our hands between our knees like Elijah on Mount Carmel calling upon the Most High who inhabiteth eternity, from which comes our help.

In the garden of Gethsemane our Lord bowed beneath the heavy load of the great sin question and in view of what was to take place at Calvary, said *"Not my will, but Thine, be done"* (Luke 22:42). He knelt under the blue Syrian sky and His soul was exceeding sorrowful and very heavy (Matt. 26:37). He was anguished at the thought of His sinless soul being brought into contact with the vileness of sin; that He must taste death for every man. An angel was dispatched from heaven to strengthen Him. As we kneel in the presence of our blessed Saviour calling upon the meritorious work of His precious blood, we receive strength from the Sanctuary.

With the children of Israel on the shores of the Red Sea we can sing: *"The Lord is my strength and song, and He is become my salvation: He is my God, and I will prepare Him an habitation; my father's God, and I will exalt Him"* (Ex. 15:2).

With David we can sing: *"The Lord is my light and my salvation; whom shall I fear? The Lord is the strength of my life; of whom shall I be afraid?"* (Ps. 27:1).

When you and I go from solitude to surrender we reach the place of divine strength; we pierce the clouds of oppression; our strength is renewed daily and we mount up, as it were, with eagle wings into God's hallowed presence and are thus enabled to let all men know whose we are and whom we serve.

SEVEN

THE GIFT OF GOD

"For by grace are ye saved through faith; and that not of your-selves: it is the gift of God: Not of works, lest any man should boast."
Ephesians 2:8

Centuries ago a circular letter was written to Christians living at Ephesus, which is Izmir now in modern Turkey. In this rich epistle, God opens His gracious heart and tells us He loved and thought of us before the foundation of the world. Secrets hidden in a past age are fully revealed and we behold heaven's wealth and earth's warfare for a people graced and gifted in the Beloved of God, the Lord Jesus Christ. The author insists that what God does and what He displays is nothing but the undeserved favour of God. Neither is the grace, nor the faith by which you partook of it, of yourselves. It is the gift of God.

PERSON

Who is this Person? The mystery hidden in God from ages and from generations, the glory and grandeur of our common faith, the rapture and rest of our adoration, is the mystery of godliness, God manifest in the flesh. The majesty of His person and the glory of His character are clearly set forth in the sacred Word.

On the very threshold of Scripture, sin raises its ugly head, plunging the cruel dagger of death into the heart of man. *"And so death passed upon all men, for that all have sinned"* (Rom. 5:12). Yet the blessed God seeing the human family in its hopelessness and helplessness, promises a Redeemer to be the Saviour of sinners (Gen. 3:15).

From this prophecy comes a growing volume of prophetic announcements. Prophet after prophet spoke of Him who was to come. Micah assures us His birth must take place at Bethlehem, over which the mystic lamp of prophecy had hung for centuries (Mic. 5:2). Nearly seven hundred and fifty years before the birth of the Saviour, a remarkable prophecy was given concerning Him. Not only did the Scriptures accurately foretell the time and conditions of His lowly birth, they foretold His character as well. Isaiah wrote concerning Him: *"His name shall be called Wonderful, Counsellor, the Mighty God, the Everlasting Father, the Prince of Peace"* (Isa. 9:6).

One recalls "the hopes and fears of all the years" that came to focus on the Babe of Bethlehem. The real message of Christmas is found in the person of Immanuel, God with us. From His incarnation issues a living hope and the promise of an eternal, triumphant life, joy beyond measure—all declared to mankind by Christ Jesus. What thrilling reading is found in Dr. Luke's narrative concerning the Christ-child. God's promises bring confidence and consolation to us all, whether in the grip of fear or the grave of despair. The Word comes anew and afresh every year, *"Fear not: for, behold, I bring you good tidings of great joy, which shall be to all people. For unto you is born this day, ... a Saviour, which is Christ the Lord"* (Luke 2:10).

PRICELESS

Again we note in reading our text that the gift of God is priceless. It is a gift infinite in worth and value, beyond money and beyond price. The things most esteemed by man, such as silver and gold, have no place in procuring salvation. The crime, the greatest of all crimes, is to think this priceless gift can be purchased. Soul salvation is not furnished on the silver and gold standard, it is by grace, and this grace is personified in the Lord Jesus Christ (John 1:17). John speaks of Him who was grace, yet Paul reveals the fullness of this grace in that wonderful verse, *"For ye know the grace of our Lord Jesus Christ, that, though he was rich, yet for your sakes he became poor, that ye through his poverty might be rich"* (2 Cor. 8:9). Of course we know that money brings much advantage, ease, comfort, power and prestige, but it does not obtain salvation.

It has been said that money is a universal provider for

everything but happiness, a passport to everywhere except heaven. Silver and gold belong to the finite, the material, the earth, and are totally unable to bring man to God. Our need is met by One who is heavenly and at the greatest cost to that person. Death to Him was the price of the gift of God. Peter tells us that it is through the precious blood of the uncreated Son of God. Christ's precious blood gives our salvation its value. How different from the world's estimate, is God's.

We are redeemed by blood and this is the appeal of the Spirit of God for consecrated living in this materialistic age. When we come to celebrate Christmas we are responsible to communicate its message to all the world.

PRESENTED

When a gift is offered it can be accepted or refused. Jesus Christ is heaven's crowning gift, far exceeding everything else that God has created. Christ is God's unspeakable gift, wrapped in heavenly love and earthly form, and presented in the gospel. Have you received God's Christmas gift? It is waiting. Have you opened your heart to Him? There was no room for Him at Bethlehem's ancient inn. Is there room for Him in your heart? Or have pleasure, ambition, self and sin so filled your heart that there is no room for Him? He stands at the door and knocks and *"as many as received Him, to them gave He the power to become the sons of God, even to them that believe on His name"* (John 1:12).

Now is the ideal time to accept this wonderful free gift. At Christmas time memories are vivid, hopes are lively, and hearts are expectant. Yet if the Saviour of the world is not central to all our thoughts and activities, memories are delusions and hopes are false. If all gifts exchanged between friends and loved ones are given other than in remembrance of the Hope of the Ages and the Desire of all nations which He has implanted in the human heart; then gifts are merely so many packages. How well it has been stated, "It is in the heart that a parcel becomes a gift." The essence of Christmas is to receive God's free gift (John 3:16). Once it is accepted, you may express your gratitude as the wise men did in worship and giving. Whatever the explanation of the gifts brought by these learned men, the challenge comes afresh to us: what are our gifts to the Saviour? The wise men are gone. We remain. What can we give?

> What shall I bring to the Saviour?
> What shall I lay at His feet?
> I have no glittering jewels,
> Gold, or frankincense sweet,
> Gifts to the Saviour I'm bringing,
> Love's richest treasures to lay,
> Low at His feet with rejoicing,
> 'Ere yonder sunset today.

We may bring the gold of sincere love. We may present the frankincense of spiritual worship. We may bring the myrrh of cleansed and consecrated lives. The gift is free and comes from the tree on which the Saviour bore our sins in His own body. It comes, so to speak, wrapped in all the love of the greatest of all givers and tied with cords of divine truth. It is personal. Will you receive God's Gift, too wonderful for words?

BETHLEHEM: WHERE ANGELS SANG

One of the most picturesque places in all the world is the little town of Bethlehem nestling in the Judean hills. A visit there is a never-to-be-forgotten experience. There is the Church of the Nativity built over the ancient rock-hewn stables that may well have been the birthplace of the Lord. There the bells of Bethlehem can be seen and heard, for their chimes are broadcasted round the world on Christmas Day. Not far away are Shepherds' fields where wandering men heard a wonderful message centuries ago. How often we enjoyed singing the oldest and the youngest Christmas carols in the same fields when we were dwelling in the land of the Bible. Whenever the word "Bethlehem" (which means "the House of Bread") comes to mind, certain memories spring to life about a Son, a Saviour, and a Sign.

A SON

In the Old Testament (see Genesis 35), we are first introduced to Bethlehem in the days of Jacob. Though he lived some 1800 years before the coming of Christ, the hand of God was on him leading him right to the House of Bread, Ephrath (another name for Bethleham). Coming along from Bethel, Jacob halted and, just on the outskirts of Bethlehem, Rachel, his beloved wife, gave birth to her second child. As she died, she cried out in pain "Benoni," which means "Son of my sorrow". Jacob called the boy, Benjamin, "Son of my right hand", and built a pillar there which remains to this day. Often I have sat by the way into Bethlehem and thought about this scene. It speaks of the birth of another Son, the Lord Jesus Christ. He was the Man of sorrows, but also the Son of God's right hand.

> He came as a babe, in the manger was laid,
> Christ Jesus the blest Son of God,
> He came from on high, that here He might die,
> To ransom us by His own blood.

A SAVIOUR

While we meditate with wonder on the birth of the little baby in a manger, we must not ever forget that He was of noble descent, for He was one of the family of David and of Abraham. The wise men knelt and worshipped him and the sky shone with a wonderful light from heaven. The beautiful name, Jesus, simply means "Jehovah the Saviour".

In the Old Testament there are three books that contain the name of Jesus—Joshua, Isaiah and Hosea. In all these books the Spirit of God has a special purpose in the meaning of the names. Joshua puts the emphasis on His person, Isaiah on His work, and Hosea on His people. So when Matthew records *"And she shall bring forth a son, and thou shalt call His name Jesus, for He shall save His people from their sins"* (Matt. 1:21), the Holy Spirit unites these three books in testimony to the Christ of God, Immanuel—"God with us".

Joshua means Saviour, and so the name of Jesus is the same as Joshua. Isaiah makes much of the work of the Redeemer and the meaning of his name is "Jehovah is Salvation". Thus, as Matthew says, our Lord came to save from sin. Finally, Hosea is another reference to the Saviour and in his book we find Jehovah's great concern for His people. So the coming of Christ was to save His people from their sins. In one verse of Scripture the Holy Spirit gathers up the teaching of the three books in the Old Testament bearing the name of Jesus. It is no wonder we sing:

> Man of sorrows, what a name
> For the Son of God who came
> Ruined sinners to reclaim:
> Hallelujah, what a Saviour.

A SIGN

From the days of David, the man after God's own heart, Bethlehem was like many other towns quietly hidden away for centuries. Then one day a mysterious star appeared in the heavens over the place where Jesus was to be born. It led the way for the wise men to come to the Babe with their gifts of gold, frankincense and myrrh. The message of the angel of the Lord was expressed in the word Saviour, which is Christ the Lord. The sign was a Baby and in this lies the mystery of the incarnation. Truly it is both mysterious and wonderful—the Son of God, the great Creator, the Lord of Glory humbling Himself to become even for a short time, the Son of man. No one in Rome, the Imperial capital, knew of His arrival and the event was not announced in the high places of the earth.

> In His birth,
> He would no glory borrow,
> No majesty from earth.

Yet He came, a Saviour long desired and long expected. And now, as the Messiah of Promise, the Lord Jehovah, God Himself, we announce Him as heaven's great gift and earth's greatest gain. Both in the Christmas season and every season, may the knowledge of His love fill our hearts with adoring worship.

NINE

JOY TO THE WORLD

Again and again, these words have been like music in our souls. Why is the Christmas message essentially one of joy? What is so unusual about the birth of Christ? How sad it is that Christians do not have a reputation for being joyful. The message of the "good news" was never meant to be seasonal. It is for the whole year.

THE MANGER

No one who has lived and dwelt in the "land of bells, yells and smells" is carried away by the picturesque displays of the manger scenes. Often I have walked around the back streets of Bethlehem where tourists never venture. There the convictions of yesterday remain the same today—that our Christmas stage effects are often misrepresented. The stable was not scrubbed, odourless or hygienic. Mary was not robed in a spotless white gown and served by angelic attendants. The stable was rough, the manger was crude, and the courtyard stank. When the Lord of Glory came to earth and the Son of God became the Son of Man, the Apostle Paul expressed it well: *Ye know the grace of our Lord Jesus Christ, that though He was rich, yet for your sakes He became poor that ye through His poverty might be rich* (2 Cor. 8:9). Just as Jesus was born in the midst of an unrenovated barn among uncouth and unregenerate society, so the Word became flesh and God was incarnate to make possible the truth:

> Born that man no more may die;
> Born to raise the sons of earth;
> Born to give them second birth

Christ comes to us as we are in all our baseness, corruptness and sinfulness—Immanuel: God with us. His communication to us: I am already here. I know your failures, your fallacies, your filth, and I am come to give you life. Let me take care of you. Why not have the real Christmas? Be merry because Christ is in your heart! In the person of the Lord Jesus Christ, God offers you the reality of life abundant and life eternal here and now. This is His promise: *"As many as received Him, to them gave He power to become the sons of God, even to them that believe on His name"* (John 1:12).

THE MESSAGE OF CHRISTMAS

If there is one time of the year when people ought to be in a jovial mood or merry in disposition it is the Yuletide season. No one enjoys me if I am sombre, disgruntled and wearing a brow of care. On Christmas Eve 1538, Martin Luther was very merry. All his words and songs and thoughts were of the incarnation of our Lord. Then with a sigh he said "Oh, we poor men, that we should be so cold and indifferent to this great joy which has been given us. This indeed is the greatest gift, and far exceeds everything else that God has created." We believe so feebly, even though the angels preach and sing. Their fair song sums up the whole of Christianity, for *"Glory to God in the highest"* is the heart of worship.

Think of what fine, happy thoughts man would have if he were not fallen. Surely the contemplation of the whole creation, and especially of the simplest grasses of the fields, proves that our Lord God is an artist like unto none. But since the pitiable fall of Adam, the Creator is dishonoured and reviled. That is why the angels summon us once more to faith in Christ, that we may give God alone the honour, and dwell in this life at peace with God and one another. Think of the Angelic message to Mary, *"And the angel came unto Mary, and said, … the Lord is with thee. … Fear not, for thou hast found favour with God"* (Luke 1:28-30).

Mary recognized that the God of all grace had blessed her above all the maidens of Israel in fulfilling through her the promise of the long-expected Messiah. Remember the angelic announcement to those shepherds as they kept watch over their flock by night? Here it is: *"Fear not: for behold, I bring you good tidings of great joy, which shall be to all people. For unto you is born this day in the city of David a Saviour, which is Christ the Lord"* (Luke 2:10-11). These matchless words are at once comprehensive and complete as to who is the Saviour and how, when, where, why and to whom He came.

What joy His coming should evoke and what gladness promote during the years yet unborn. These words of the angel are so familiar we have lost their freshness, felicity and fullness. It was a message concerning a Saviour not an advisor, not a mere teacher, not simply a social reformer, not only an example, but a deliverer. In a time of national crisis in Israel when Saul and his people faced the taunts of the Philistine giant, a shepherd boy born in Bethlehem came to their rescue and delivered them out of the hand of their enemies.

Centuries later David's greater Son defeated him who had the power of death, the devil, and until this day the place is known as Golgotha, *"the place of the skull."* God's Deliverer, typified in David, had come and by the cross had conquered. Thus the message of the gospel is prefigured in the Old Testament. Again the Christmas message is predicted by the prophets. There are three hundred and thirty-three specific predictions concerning the Lord Jesus Christ and upwards of three hundred of these were fulfilled at His first coming.

Consider:
1. Bethlehem, the place of His birth foretold by Micah 700 years before it occurred (Mic. 5:2).
2. Christ rode *"upon a colt, the foal of an ass"* (Matt. 21:4-11) as was foretold by Zechariah 500 years before the Saviour came (Zech. 9:9).
3. In Isaiah chapter 53, the purpose and passion of Christ is set forth as nowhere else in the Scriptures, 700 years in advance (1 Pet. 2:21-24).
4. The same prophet also predicted (Isa. 53:12) how He would be *"numbered with the transgressors"* (Mark 15:28).
5. His garments were disposed of (John 19:23-24) exactly as the psalmist depicted 1000 years earlier (Ps. 22:18).

6. Contrary to all custom, His bones were left unbroken (John 19:33) as had been anticipated for a millennium (Ps. 34:20).
7. His glorious resurrection (John 20), though not believed by all, was prophesied 1000 years in advance (Ps. 16:10).

What a message was proclaimed by angels from heaven. It was a night of unparalleled brilliance. The news was to be blessed to untold millions and never had the hosts of heaven such unspeakable praise, saying: *"Glory to God in the highest, and on earth peace, good will toward men"* (Luke 2:14).

THE MARVEL

The marvel of Christmas is the mystery of the incarnation. It was indeed a unique act of God in bringing to birth the Saviour of the world. Christ was born not for a select people, but for all people regardless of colour, class or condition. The gospel meets the need of all nationalities, Asian, African or European. With God there is no first world, second world and third world for, *"God so loved the world, that He gave his only begotten Son, that whosoever believeth in him should not perish, but have everlasting life"* (John 3:16).

What a thrill to preach such a message for it is the remedy for all this world's woes, and the solution for all its complex problems. The gospel is the answer to its questions whether social, political, cultural, commercial or national. Does the Christian message inspire joy in your life? Are you a joyless person? Do you possess the holy joy of the Lord or has materialism robbed you of the message of the Christmas season? Oh! the wonder of such a message until this hour which meets the need of business men, military men, the religious leaders and their followers, young revolutionaries and feminists, and people of every kindred, tribe and nation.

The gospel is God's power unto salvation to every one who has believed (Rom. 1:16). Let us follow the example of the shepherds of Bethlehem who *"returned glorifying God."* All their joy and expectation centered in Christ the Saviour who was born. In the midst of all the Christmas festivities, let us be marked by gladness and seek to fulfill the words *"in all things He might have the preeminence"* (Col. 1:18). Make sure Christ is born in your heart and this will make every day full of unspeakable joy and glory.

OUT OF HIS FULLNESS

The text before me, *"Out of His fullness have all we received, and grace for grace"* (John 1:16), was wondrously illuminated by a recent visit to one of the greatest natural wonders of the world, Victoria Falls, in Central Africa. On November 16, 1853, David Livingstone emerged from the thick bush and gazed with awe into the deep wide chasm into which this mighty river thundered. Amazed and astounded at what he saw and almost deafened by the roar, he named the falls after his beloved sovereign, "The Victoria Falls". The the picturesque name of the Africans was *Mosi-oa-Tunya* ("the smoke that thunders").

Over the years the beauty of the falls, which changes throughout the season with the flow of the Zambezi River, has been preserved by a band of dedicated men whose task it is to preserve the natural phenomena as in the day of the explorer, Livingstone. Great clouds of spray often obscure the giant walls of water pouring over the chasm, but the rainbow is always seen at some time during the sun-lit days. Until today there are no bright neon lights, no steel railings, concrete paths, not even a coca-cola stand—just nature in all her glory and pristine beauty. How apt the words of the discoverer, "scenes so lovely must have been gazed upon by angels in their flight."

Sitting near the falls when the Zambezi was at its height, I read my Bible in spite of the curtain of mist all about me. The Holy Spirit directed my heart to the above beautiful text and gazing with reverence on the 75 million gallons of water hurtling over the brink, I heard God's voice and worshipped before the vision. As long as life shall last we can be assured of the fullness, richness, limitless exhaustlessness of our resources in Christ. Further, the rainbow reminded me that His promises are fixed, final and forever because of Christ who has revealed the hand and heart of God. Surely the knowledge of God's provision and His promise ought to stir our hearts to worship and our lips to exclaim, "O Lord my God, how great Thou art." Do you know Him?

All Christians have eternal life, but not all Christians have abundant life. There can be life without health; there can be movement without progress. There may be war, but not defeat. We may serve and never succeed. We may try and never triumph. It is one thing to possess eternal life and another to lay hold on eternal life and daily experience the perpetual dew of the Holy Spirit which communicates life, freshness and power. Abundant life is fullness of life in the power of the Holy Spirit. God offers salvation to the lost through the death of Jesus Christ, as a free gift, and to all who are true believers in Him, He offers the fullness of the Holy Spirit. It is not merely a second blessing. It is a third blessing, a hundredth blessing, a thousandth blessing. There are many ways to describe the life of fullness. It is synonymous to say, be emptied of yourself; surrender your will to the Lord; rejoice in the One whom you have trusted as Saviour. Yield yourself to Him as Lord and Master. Give your life to Him. Any of these phrases may cover the basis of the experience in your life, providing you follow the full implication of surrender, of yieldedness. Christ must be enthroned as Lord of all.

Then the Spirit comes in His gentle fullness to bring His fruit, *"Love, joy, peace, longsuffering, gentleness, goodness, faith, meekness, self control"* (Gal. 5:21-22). Then He brings that which the world seeks and never finds: quiet contentment in the midst of sorrow, true fellowship with all of the Lord's own, lips that open in His witness, a purse that is open in his cause, a heart that is strong to do great things for Him. In short, it is a life that is hid with Christ in God and manifests Christ wherever it may please Him to direct our steps.

ELEVEN

RUNNER FROM THE LONG GRASS

In central Africa, Yotham Muleya will always be remembered as the barefoot African youth who, to everyone's amazement, beat the great Empire runner, Gordon Pirie, in Salisbury. He was the trailblazer in opening up the field of sport to the individual, regardless of his colour. In Gordon Pirie's book, *"Running Wild"*, he has this to say about the track star:

> He was a quiet, charming fellow and an excellent runner. I met him a couple of days before the meeting and advised him on points about the three-mile race in which we were to appear. I was the one who suggested he should race with bare feet.

The ceremonies prior to the race were over. Each runner was at the starting line, tense, ready to begin the three-mile struggle for victory. Off they went. One mile—two miles and, unbelievably, the barefoot African was leading. "What's his name?" excited spectators asked each other. "Muleya—Yotham Muleya." They neared the finish line and Muleya was still in front. The British champion was fighting hard, but Muleya pulled even farther ahead and finally won by one hundred yards. All the people were astonished and the cheers were heard and heralded from the Zambezi to the Limpopo.

The slightly built African's triumph went much further than the record book. A great African athlete had cracked the race barrier in federal athletics. The crack started by Muleya's victory is still widening, and his achievement will continue to inspire youths of all lands in the interests of international goodwill and sportsmanship.

It was not long before the fame of Muleya spread across the country and almost every village and school boy knew about the runner from the long grass of Mudukula. Much publicity and distinction came to this splendid youth, yet he was unmoved and continued as a humble student working towards a vocational certificate at the technical college in Lusaka. Here I became acquainted with the runner and, though he had a rigorous training schedule and much desk work, he always attended the regular weekly Bible class. How well I recall when giving a talk on Bible names, he questioned the name, Yotham. I explained that it meant "Jehovah is perfect" and went on to tell how a King of Judah of the same name lived a consistent life before the Lord (2 Chron. 27:6). I was greatly encouraged when he replied, "I would like to live right and be an influence in my country." On another occasion, he remained at the close of a Bible lecture and sincerely affirmed his faith in Christ. I found there was also a definite desire on his part to know the Word of God.

Soon after the summer break from college, Muleya, with another student athlete, was on his way to the U.S.A. under the International Educational Exchange Program of the State Department. He was to be abroad three months in specialized training and coaching at Central Michigan University. A full schedule of competition would greatly improve Muleya's time for the one-mile and three-mile runs.

In less than a week after arriving in America, the African track trailblazer had run his last race. Three miles south of Mount Pleasant, Michigan in rainy weather, the car in which he was riding skidded out of control and crossed into the path of an on-coming car. There was a horrible crash and five hours later Yotham Muleya, the ambassador athlete from the Choma district 7,000 miles away, was dead.

People in both America and Africa were stunned and the personal loss was felt by all. More than 1,000 people of all races, great and small, paid their last tribute to Muleya at his funeral at Choma and held a memorial service at his college. It was a privilege under God for this author to give the message on the college campus using the text *"He being dead, yet speaketh"* (Heb. 11:4).

From near and far tributes came concerning Yotham Muleya's

place in the world of sports: "Great athlete as he was, it was the man and his character that we loved. His unshakable modesty, his integrity and personal simplicity were completely unaffected by his dramatic and richly deserved fame. He has an important place in the history of Central Africa." Another said, "Muleya made his great contribution as one of the builders of a new nation, and generations yet unborn will not forget him. He was a pioneer of multi-racialism in athletics, and by his own splendid performance on the sports-field advanced the cause of his fellows far more effectively and rapidly than any politician could ever hope to do."

It seems but yesterday that, as the village cattle grazed peacefully in the surrounding bush, a small gathering stood with bowed heads around the grave of Yotham Muleya on the hillside outside the tiny village. From the twisting stony road which led us through the Zambezi escarpment to the village where Yotham had been born, the water of the mighty Kariba Lake was visible in the misty background. Here in this peaceful setting, the body of Muleya was buried and now over the grave a beautiful headstone has been erected with a bronze plaque bearing the words, *"So run, that ye may obtain"* (1 Cor. 9:24).

Muleya with his broad smile, satchel in hand, and farewell wave will forever live in memory as well as on film. But far more important, today he lives in heaven. He also lives in our home, because we named our son after our beloved friend, the runner from the long grass. Our prayer to God is that you who read this brief account of Yotham Muleya's shining testimony may run the great race of faith and take hold of eternal life through Jesus Christ our Lord.

The following testimony of Yotham Muleya, obtained while visiting him in the Copper Belt, has not been told nearly as much as the one about his victories at the Salisbury Stadium, and yet it is far more important.

> I am glad I know the Lord Jesus Christ as my own personal Saviour. Since that hour when the preacher read from the Gospel of St. John, chapter three, verse sixteen: *"For God so loved the world, that he gave his only begotten Son that whosoever believeth in Him should not*

perish, but have everlasting life" and switched on my mind again to the book of Isaiah, chapter fifty-three verse six, *"All we like sheep have gone astray; we have turned every one to his own way: and the Lord hath laid on him the iniquity of us all,"* my mind and heart were moved to accept Christ. I then felt the presence of God and His Spirit speaking to my soul and at that very moment I accepted Christ as my Lord and Saviour, and I was illuminated with joy for I became a new man with broad smiles (2 Cor. 5:17). From personal experience, I can say that there is no better way of life; and only true success and prosperity is found by abiding in Christ. My belief in the Lord Jesus has changed my whole outlook, and in any ventures and victories; in study or sport, I am dependent on Christ. I joined the career of Physical Sociology because the Lord is my Shepherd, and in my witness I shall not want, for He also is my refuge, fortress, shield and buckler. I long to be a good and faithful witness for Christ, and for all you who read this testimony I am wondering how long you will continue to leave him out of your life. Without Christ there is nothing but disappointment here and desolation hereafter. To be a Christian is life with a purpose and for all who run with patience there is a prize at the end and, in the present, the life that wins every time.

—Yotham Muleya

TWELVE

THE SHADOW OF A GREAT ROCK

"And a man shall be as an hiding place from the wind, and a covert from the tempest; as rivers of water in a dry place, as the shadow of a great rock in a weary land."

Isaiah 32:2

One of the most scenic settings of any city on earth is Table Mountain. It is a controlling factor in the weather pattern of the country and also central to the city of Cape Town, often referred to as the Tavern of the Seas, and the Mother City of South Africa. Though the Cape has changed hands many times, the Rock endures and is a landmark from generation to generation. The panoramic view from the summit of the mountain is awe inspiring looking out to the Atlantic and Indian Oceans. How eagerly we scanned the shore line as the mountain came into focus some 200 kilometres out to sea. We shall never forget coming face to face with the mountain as it rises in a sheer rocky precipice until it levels off like a table top and salutes the circular arms known as Devil's Peak, Lion's Head and Signal Hill.

Sometimes on a cloudy day we cannot see the mountain, yet it is always there. So in the shadows and mists of life when faith is so sorely tried, we know that God is still on the throne and we can endure as seeing Him who is invisible. Just as Table Mountain has been a world landmark since the 15th century, so the Bible declares the "Rock" is one of the titles of Jehovah found frequently on the pages of the Book of Books.

Centuries ago Moses lamented that Israel forsook God and lightly esteemed the Rock of his Salvation (Deut. 32:15). He is the Mighty Rock whose shadow is cast over a heat-stricken and weary land. To whom could this lofty rugged figure apply but One who is the Rock of Ages through which no scorching rays could penetrate? Who but He could give rest, refreshment and refuge from the storm blasts that sweep over our lives? Isaiah, whose very name can be freely rendered "Jesus Saves", lived during the stormy period of the Assyrian invasion.

In a magnificent disclosure he presents Jesus as a Rock in a weary land, a shelter in the time of storm. Often when walking along the beach, jogging or driving towards Cape Town, I would lift up my eyes to the Rock and learn that stones have a message. The Rock is a constant reminder of the faithfulness of God. The Rock is the symbol of stability, strength, and sufficency.

STABILITY

Isaiah knew something of tyranny and oppression in his day and he looks forward in his prophecy to the coming of the Messiah who will judge the world in righteousness, and the people in equity. How reassuring to know the Rock can never be moved out of His place (Job 18:4). The Rock on which our faith rests cannot be shaken or moved though floods may come and winds beat upon it. To the Christian, Christ is the Foundation Stone (Eph. 2:20). To the Jew, Christ is the Stumbling Stone at his first coming, but the Headstone of the Corner at His second coming (Rom. 9:33; Zech. 4:7). To the Gentile world powers, Christ will yet be the Smiting Stone cut out without hands (Dan. 2:34). To the non-Christian, Christ will be the Crushing Stone of Judgment (Matt. 21:44).

STRENGTH

How impressive to behold the Cape Rock and know it will outlast the storms of time. Waters will not wash it away, nor winds remove the landmark of the Peninsula. It towers high above man and for generations has been a landmark. Our Lord is the One who is the Mighty God steadfast through time, the same yesterday and today and forever (Isa. 9:6; Heb. 13:8). He is seated at God's right hand and lives to save and help all who come to Him. How solemn to realize that those who are not built upon the Rock will be shattered by it. *"And whosoever shall fall on this Stone shall be broken,"* said Christ pointing to Himself, *"but on whomsoever it shall fall, it will grind him to powder"* (Matt. 21:44).

SUFFICIENCY

This signifies sufficiency in the day of trouble and tragedy. Moses knew something of this when he took refuge in the cleft of the Rock (Ex. 33:22). David was aware of the preciousness of the Rock as a hiding place (Ps. 18:2). Elijah, in the day of weariness and wickedness, actually heard the voice of the Rock (1 Kgs. 19:11-12). In the eternal Rock of Ages there is water (Ex. 17:6), there is honey (Ps. 81:16), there is singing (Isa. 42:11), there is standing (Ps. 40:2), there is oil (Deut. 32:13), and there is rest (Isa. 32:2). Yes, there is more than enough for all in the Rock. But how costly!

Over nineteen hundred years ago the Lord of Glory was smitten that the Spirit of Life might flow from Him to all who drink (Ex. 17:6; 1 Cor. 10:4; John 4:13-14). Out from the crucified, now glorified, Saviour flowed the water, a beautiful type of the Holy Spirit, the gift of God. Of Israel we read: *"they did all drink the same spiritual drink"* (1 Cor. 10:4). And believers today have been made *"to drink of one Spirit"* (1 Cor. 10:4, RV). This is the birthright and the heritage of every member of the family of God.

As in the land of the Bible, so in Africa there are many stones and mountainous passes. It is no wonder the prophets and shepherds found in the rocks and hills emblems of their God, their Refuge and Saviour. Is your house built on the Rock? Have your feet been set upon that Rock? Jesus is the only One who can lift you out of the mire of sin. Have you found in Christ peace and rest, a refuge, a remedy and a repose from the passing storm to be able to sing:

> Rock of Ages, cleft for me,
> Let me hide myself in thee…

Why not pray if such is your spiritual condition? *"When my heart is overwhelmed; lead me to the Rock that is higher than I"* (Ps. 61:2). Can you say personally, *"The Lord is my rock and my fortress"* (Ps. 18:2)?

THIRTEEN

PRAYER GIVES POWER

In Isaiah we read, *"There is none that calleth upon Thy name, that stirreth up himself to take hold of Thee"* (Isa. 64:7). In the literal Hebrew, the word means to rouse oneself out of a sleep or sloth, and take hold with intensity on Jehovah, to call on God with every fibre of one's being. Victory in the prayer life of the believer is exceedingly costly. Those who have ever done anything for God know something of the value of prayer. They have been men and women who did not shrink from the light God manifested with their Calvary experience as the place of death. Their's is a richer, deeper and fuller life of power with God and men. These were men who paid the price for prayer and power, and God withheld nothing from them.

Surely the pathway to power, peace and prosperity is to use our knees and call upon God without ceasing, knowing, *"the power available—dynamic in its working"* (Jas. 5:16 AMPLIFIED). Prayer was the breath of life to the first century Christians.

- Moses prayed and the enemy was defeated.
- Joshua prayed and the sun stood still.
- Elijah prayed and the rain stayed.
- Isaiah prayed and received his commission.
- Daniel prayed and was delivered from danger.
- Nehemiah prayed and the way to Jerusalem was opened.

Lord, teach me how to pray! It worked in the days of Peter and Paul; in the days of George Müller, John Wesley and David Livingstone. It works today.

FOURTEEN

SALVATION SO SIMPLE

Could it be that some casual reader of this little book has yet to fully understand just what the gospel is all about? The questions we now seek to answer are so simple, yet so important! Consider the following with great care; your very life depends on it.

WHY DO I NEED SALVATION?

I have a GREAT NEED.

1. God is holy and cannot look on sin. God is holy and no sin will ever enter His presence (Hab. 1:13). *"The Lord our God is holy"* (Ps. 99:9).
2. Man is sinful: *"For all have sinned, and come short of the glory of God"* (Rom 3:23). You must know God's standard before you will realize your own status. You will not want a doctor unless you know you are sick. You will not want a rescuer unless you know you are drowning. God's book says, *"All we like sheep have gone astray; we have turned every one to his own way"* (Isa. 53:6).
3. Sin separates man from God. No person, even if he has committed only one sin in his life, can reach heaven because of that sin. *"But your iniquities have separated between you and your God, and your sins have hid His face from you"* (Isa. 59:2).
4. It is utterly impossible for man to save himself, whether by keeping the Golden Rule, living up to the Ten Commandments, praying night or day, being baptized or joining the church, even doing the best you can. Your own works will never save you (Rom. 3:19-20).

HOW DO I GET SALVATION?

I have GOOD NEWS.

1. Acknowledge before God that you are a sinner, and turn to the Lord Jesus Christ in true repentance.
2. Believe the message of the cross, for it is good N.E.W.S. for all men—North and East and West and South.
3. The Lord Jesus came from heaven and died for our sins at Calvary; He rose again from the dead and is living today. You must accept by faith this same Lord Jesus as your personal Saviour.

WHO CAN GIVE SALVATION?

I have a GIFT NOW.

1. You need wait no longer, *"Behold, now is the accepted time; behold, now is the day of salvation"* (2 Cor. 6:2).
2. God says there is salvation in none other person except the Lord Jesus (Acts 4:12). It is a gift from God (Eph. 2:8-10). So then neither Mohammed, nor Buddha, nor Confucius, nor the church—Protestant, Catholic, Greek Orthodox—but only a Person can save you (Matt. 1:21). Morality, philanthropy, pleasing personality are all filthy rags in the sight of God (Isa. 64:6). A Saviour is needed for your sin (John 14:6; Mark 2:17). Do not delay, for the road by-and-by leads to the town called never. Don't wait till you are a better person, for Christ came to call sinners: there are none righteous (Rom. 3:10). Systems and sanctuaries, rites and ceremonies, pilgrimages and payments are inadequate. Salvation is of the Lord, and in God's Son, the living resurrected Christ, is found security, safety, and satisfaction. I have received the Lord Jesus Christ in this way. Will you?

WHAT DO I GAIN BY SALVATION?

I have a GLORIOUS NEVER.

1. I shall **never** perish (John 3:16).
2. I shall **never** be snatched out of God's hand (John 10:28-29).

3. I shall **never** be forsaken by God (Heb. 13:5).
4. I shall **never** be separated from the love of God (Rom. 8:39).

THE COLLECTED WRITINGS OF LES RAINEY

This Second Volume of *The Collected Writings of Les Rainey* contains his three **Old Testement commentaries**:

The Bible in Brief:
The Old Testament

A Syllabus of the Scriptures:
The Old Testament

Biographies of
The Old Testament

Binding: Paper
Size: 5.5" X 8.5"
Genre: Bible Study/ Commentary

This Third Volume of *The Collected Writings of Les Rainey* contains his three **New Testement commentaries**:

The Bible in Brief:
The New Testament

A Syllabus of the Scriptures:
The New Testament

Biographies of
The New Testament

Binding: Paper
Size: 5.5" X 8.5"
Genre: Bible Study/ Commentary

Les Rainey

Born in 1914 in Brantford, Ontario, Canada. Born Again while attending an Inter-Varsity Camp in Northern Ontario. Baptized and received into assembly fellowship at Bethel Chapel, Brantford, Ontario. Commended by the assembly to the work of the Lord, who he has faithfully served for over half a century. Les was trained at Dallas Theological Seminary, the University of Edinburg, the King's College of London, and the Hebrew University in Jerusalem. He served the Lord as a missionary to: Bermuda, Israel, and Africa for over 50 years, which included time in Kenya, Zambia, Zimbabwe and Botswana. Les has traveled extensively preaching and teaching the Word of God. At present he is living in August, GA. USA.

304 Killaly St. West | Port Colborne | ON | L3K 6A6 | Canada | 1 800 952 2382 | E-mail: info@gospelfolio.com | www.gospelfolio.com

Printed in the United States
107805LV00003B/16-39/A